Britannia Street

Beth Cox

LEAF BY LEAF

Published by Leaf by Leaf
an imprint of Cinnamon Press
www.cinnamonpress.com

The right of Beth Cox to be identified as author of this work has been asserted by him in accordance with the Copyright, Designs and Patent Act, 1988. © 2021, Beth Cox

ISBN 978-1-78864-929-2

British Library Cataloguing in Publication Data. A CIP record for this book can be obtained from the British Library.

Designed and typeset in Adobe Jensen by Cinnamon Press.

Cover design by Adam Craig © Adam Craig.

Cinnamon Press is represented by Inpress

Acknowledgements

Thank to Jan Fortune and Adam Craig for bringing *Britannia Street* to the world. Thanks also to all who read the manuscript, David, Alison, Joanne and Rachel, Deborah Grace, Theresa Taylor and Judith Godfrey. Thanks to Sarah-Clare Conlon for her editing. Sally Cline's mentorship was invaluable in encouraging me to keep going. Thanks also to my tutor Geoff Ryman and Professor Jeanette Winterson at the Centre for New Writing at Manchester University for their suggestions and support.

To David

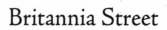

Britannia Street

Part 1

Chapter 1

Great-aunt Annie's Table

Can a table hold secrets? And then give them up? Well, that's what happened in 1964. I was eighteen and already married. I had inherited the table from Great-aunt Annie. My parents and I sat around the table, drinking tea. Mother touched the varnished tabletop.

'It's not in bad condition,' she said. 'I think it'll be all right for you.'

My father passed his hands over the table and partway down the two legs nearest to him. It was as if he was caressing it, massaging it, encouraging it to let out the truth. He stood and walked around it, carefully looking at it.

'It will open out and make a longer table,' he said. 'You just pull out the sides and lift up the middle.'

Mother and I stood up holding our mugs, so he could demonstrate. It fell into place easily, making a table twice its original size.

'I bet that's not been opened for a long time,' said Mother. 'It'll be really useful.'

We all sat around the extended table. We smiled at each other. We sat there expectantly. Waiting. And this was when the table began to give up its secrets.

'Annie was the last of her generation,' said Father. 'It was a different world when she was born in 1886. It's a sad story.' He looked at Mother.

'You'd better tell her the full story, Harold,' said Mother.

'When we cleared out Annie's house, we found her birth certificate… and there's a space where her father's name should be.'

'Oh,' I said. 'So, what does that mean?'

Father took a deep breath then sighed. 'Aunt Annie and her brother Albert, my father, your grandfather, were both illegitimate—we don't know who Annie and Albert's father was—or even if they had the same father,' he said.

'It was a terrible thing in those days,' said Mother. 'Annie felt it all her life... the shame of it, then your great-grandmother Elizabeth married John Goulburn, they left Lancaster and came to Bolton, and Annie and Albert changed their surnames to Cox.'

I looked at my parents. What? This made no sense to me.

'Be thankful they did, Beth, otherwise you would have been Beth Cock,' said Father.

'Are you saying their name was Cock, spelt C-O-C-K, and not Cox?'

'Yes, Annie Cock, born in Lancaster,' said Father. 'It's on her birth certificate.'

'You're right, I'm glad they did change it,' I said with a giggle.

'Annie never got over being illegitimate. She was ashamed—it's the family secret, left behind in Lancaster with their old surname when they came to Bolton,' said Father.

I felt a tug of connection with this woman, Annie's mother, my great-grandmother, who, it seems, had brought shame on the family. I'd done something similar myself and although times were changing in the early 1960s, there was still a musty odour of Victorian prurience in the air. Mrs. Caldwell, the butcher's wife, didn't speak to me when I got pregnant. She couldn't even look at me as we passed in the street. If you weren't a 1950s ideal housewife wearing a neat apron over a full-skirted dress, with a short, tidy hairstyle, cooking your husband's dinner in a modern kitchen, after your white, church wedding, you were not socially acceptable. You should certainly not get pregnant when you're sixteen and unmarried.

'Her parents threw her out,' said Mother.

'That's awful,' I said. 'Poor woman.'

'That's how it was in those days,' said Father.

I was washing up after they left. I remembered that when I was about eight or nine, I stayed with Great-aunt Annie and her husband George one weekend. They lived in an old-fashioned house, which still had gas mantles in the hallway left over from the days before people had electricity in their houses. It was an adventure for me, the first time sleeping away from home. I played draughts with George and he taught me how to spell 'phlegm'. George and Annie had a front room which was never used. It had a display cabinet in one corner which was full of little china ornaments. I liked to kneel on the floor and peer into it. It was during that visit that I noticed there was an old photograph above the cabinet in an ornate gold frame. It was of a woman who looked like Aunt Lizzy, my father's sister. She was wearing an old-fashioned dark dress. I asked Great-aunt Annie who it was.

'It's my mother,' she said. 'She was called Elizabeth, like you.'

'What was your name before you married Uncle George?' I said.

'Goulburn, Annie Goulburn,' she said.

This answer had puzzled me because I knew Aunt Annie was Grandad Cox's sister, so shouldn't she have been called Annie Cox? I think I asked her and didn't get a satisfactory reply because I know I did ask my parents. I was fobbed off by them. They gave each other one of those what-do-we-say-now glances and I knew I had hit on something they didn't want me to know. But I had a strong sense of this being important, something I must remember. I knew they weren't going to say any more at that time.

So, I forgot it, although not completely—it was always there in a box somewhere in the further recesses of my mind, which would become full of other boxes over the years. Boxes labelled 'husband', 'children', 'work', 'friends', 'shopping', 'cooking', 'washing' and 'miscellaneous'—until now, 2004, that is. I decided back then that I must ask more about it some time. But it stayed behind that growing

11

number of boxes until it was too late to ask. This is my search for the truth behind this story and the meaning of it for me three generations later.

Chapter 2
Breakdown 2004

It is over forty years since that conversation around Great-aunt Annie's table. Forty years in which I have not felt ready or able to begin the search for evidence of my ancestors' lives in Victorian Lancaster. I have always known I would undertake this research and from time to time I have stored away more snippets of conversations and references to my ancestors that held clues and information that I knew would be useful. In 1990 when my youngest daughter Rebecca went to university in London, I asked her if she would be willing to search the archives for Grandad Cox's birth certificate. She agreed and provided the first concrete evidence that confirmed what I had been told. But I still didn't undertake any further research. I was too busy. I had three daughters, a husband and a full-time job as a nurse, a nurse tutor and later a psychotherapist. Until the advent of the Internet, documents were archived in London and I had no idea how I might go about the research. I put it on hold, but I wonder now if I was avoiding something, because it was only after experiencing a depressive breakdown that I began to think seriously about undertaking the research.

I'm a therapist so I know about other people's breakdowns, but when I was having one of my own, I did what I knew others sometimes did; I tried to ignore it and work through it. For the kind of therapy I trained in—psychoanalytic psychotherapy—the trainee is required to undertake therapy themselves and I had, but there remained an area of my psyche that I knew had not been explored. I hadn't withheld information from my therapist—I had talked about my past—it was more that the focus and priorities at that time were different.

Several events came together which contributed to cause my depression. My marriage had not been easy at times. We

13

grew apart. My husband no longer loved me, and I left him. I had a disastrous love affair. I was alone and the world in which I'd taken pleasure seemed a hostile place. I became exhausted and I no longer wanted to go outside my home. I couldn't make decisions and I couldn't concentrate. I took time off work and I rested. But I didn't improve, I cried all the time. I couldn't smile. I couldn't sleep. I was getting worse. Life didn't seem worth living and when I began to think about how I might kill myself, I knew I must see my doctor. Suicidal ideation is the medical term for it. I had it.

A breakdown signals the need for change. I retired from my job and wound down my private practice. I have been looking after people since I was thirteen and I can no longer do that. I am scared. I lost myself and although I have now stopped crying, am sleeping better, and functioning well enough in the world, I know I haven't completely recovered. I need to discover who I am behind the roles of mother, wife, daughter, nurse, therapist, and rebuild myself, put myself first. As I emerge from the bleak place I had fallen into, propped up by anti-depressants, I find myself thinking more about the family history. I have a strong feeling that there is something in it I need to discover. It's not a rational academic interest, it's an emotional, visceral compulsion. In order to find myself today, I need to know where I have come from, who my ancestors were and what that means for me.

There is only one other person left on my father's side of the family besides me. My cousin Margaret, the daughter of my father's eldest sister, Aunty Elsie. My father was one of four children. He was born in between Aunty Elsie and Aunty Lizzy. He also had a younger brother, Cyril who was killed in the Second World War. Now, with my father's generation all gone, and just Margaret and I remaining my compulsion is deepened and strengthened. I am doing this for myself, but this search is overlayered by the need for others to know Elizabeth. This is also for my great-grandmother and for our descendants, otherwise the story will die with me. I asked Cousin Margaret if she knew anything about the family history. I told her a bit of what I knew. It was the first she had heard of this story and I'm not sure she believed me, even though I had evidence.

I have the copy of my grandfather's birth certificate, that Rebecca managed to find in the archives in London. It shows that Albert Edward Cock, boy, was born on 27th March 1876. His mother's name was Elizabeth Cock. There was that blank space under the heading 'Father' that my own father had alluded to. The address was 10 Britannia Street, Lancaster. I felt sad as I read the words on the copy of the birth certificate in my hand. I imagined Elizabeth all alone in Britannia Street, giving birth. Who would have looked after her? It was Elizabeth who had registered the birth on 15th April. There must have been no one else to do it for her. Another column was labelled Name, Surname and Maiden Surname of Mother. She had written Cock, her maiden name. No married name, no father's name; there was no hiding in Victorian England. The birth certificate saw to that. I imagined the disapproving looks she might have received when she went to the Registrar's office. If her family would have nothing to do with her, how on earth did she live?

The later name change to Cox suggests that the surname Cock had the same connotations then as now. No wonder they changed it when they had the chance. And her name was Elizabeth. The same as mine. I have always been called Beth, but my name is Elizabeth. We have the same name. A cold finger from the past touched me. I shivered. I had disturbed something. I put the certificate in a safe place. I did not see Cousin Margaret often, she lived in another part of the country. It was a few years later when I showed her Grandad's birth certificate. She said again, 'Are you sure? I've never heard any of this.'

What happened in Victorian Lancaster, a long time ago? Something so shameful that it had to be buried and forgotten as if it never happened. But it's forcing its way out of the box in my mind. I've moved the box to the forefront, and I've begun to take things out of it. And something strange is happening. I'm developing another obsession alongside the family history. I'm constantly thinking about my teenage years, the four years from twelve to sixteen specifically, which came to define my life. I can't stop the memories as they flood, remarkably clearly and detailed, into my mind. They're in a box adjacent to the Lancaster story. As a therapist I know it's not so strange, I have struggled with my past, I have never really come to terms with it despite my therapy while I was training. In that therapy there were too many other unresolved issues to deal with, not least the fact that I hadn't grieved for the loss of both my parents, and to some extent my brother John, when I was in my twenties. I cried and talked about them for years in therapy and I have some peace about those issues; as far as anyone can deal with such catastrophic loss, I have done so. Now it's time for *myself*, the self that has been buried beneath all my roles in life. I know I need to understand the teenage Beth, what drove her, what motivated her. That teenage Beth is me, a part of me that I've tried to live down, to cover up, to deny even. I know at the deepest level of my being that my family history carries meanings that are connected to those four years when my own family disintegrated. Not only am I obsessed with these two time periods, but since retirement I have time and the Internet on my side. Many records are now online. No more excuses. The time has come to face it.

Chapter 3
The End of Childhood 1958

It was not long after my twelfth birthday, in January 1958, that the first of several changes and traumas occurred that made me think the world had suffered a seismic shift. It was as if I went to bed one night and woke up the following day to a world that was turning in the wrong direction. It first showed itself when a move to a new house was decreed by my parents. It was that move that precipitated the changes in our fortunes.

Before the move, I remember an enchanted childhood, when the summers were sunny and I played outside in the wood behind our houses with my friend Joy, who lived next door; when we took picnics into the nearby park and saw kingfishers flash iridescent turquoise over streams. Father had a successful business as a furniture manufacturer. Mother was busy cooking, cleaning, washing and ironing. She helped at my father's business when they were busy. They'd met when they were both apprentices at Waring & Gillow's, a highly regarded Manchester and Lancaster furniture business. When they married in 1935, they set up their own business making furniture and soft furnishings, in Bolton, where my father came from. My brother John was born in 1937 and I followed nine years later in 1945, after the War. We both went to Bolton School, a Direct Grant Grammar School, with the boys' and girls' divisions strictly separate. We had friends and relatives close by. Our home was a semi-detached house in a leafy green suburb. It was a 1950s dream, although not a dream usually associated with a town in Lancashire, whose fortunes were declining as the cotton trade was dying. But we didn't all wear flat caps and clogs. There were many pleasant areas in Bolton as well as the old mills, terraced houses and cobbles.

Beneath the perfect surface of our lives lay a reality that

was different. My father was often ill; he was delicate, sensitive. He could also be harsh—violent even—and I felt his hand slapping my legs whenever he and I were in conflict. There were regular clashes between Father and John. Father would criticise John's table manners, his voice harsh and loud. There was one disturbing occasion when I saw Father throw a book he'd taken from John on to the fire. John stood by watching. I screamed at Father.

'Why are you burning a book? You love books.'

'It's rubbish,' he said.

I ran into the kitchen where Mother was and told her. I cried as she put her arm around me and told me to leave them alone. Mother did not show her feelings much. There were arguments when Father threatened to leave, or threatened to break plates and dishes. He never did, but the threat was terrifying, because he could also be loving, kind and playful. He made up funny stories about the neighbours and our relatives. One featured the rather snobby lady next door getting her big toe caught in the washing wringers. I laughed and laughed at that one. I have fond and happy memories of Sunday afternoon walks with him, just the two of us walking through Moss Bank Park, through the village of Barrow Bridge with its stream and pretty cottages, and up the sixty-three steps, which had to be counted every single time. At the top lay a bluebell wood which sloped down to a stream. There was a boating lake at Barrow Bridge, and a shop selling candyfloss and ice cream. A small child's version of heaven.

One day in February 1958, I was helping Mother to make tea.

'Beth,' said Mother as she buttered bread. 'Will you set the table please when you've finished making the custard—your father will be here soon.'

'The custard's ready,' I said. I laid out the cutlery.

'Your father hates driving backwards and forwards to Accrington, so we're thinking of moving to... be closer to his work.'

'Move,' I said. I was shocked by this idea. 'We can't move, I like it here.' This was wrong: this house was our home, our lives were here in this house, in this place. My father had sold his furniture business a year or two before. He'd suffered from 'nerves' so he sold it and bought another business in Accrington. This business was a wholesale stationers. In time this business was to prove equally stressful.

'I know, but your father can't carry on, it's nearly thirty miles, sixty miles a day.' Mother put the plate of bread and butter on the kitchen table. 'It takes at least an hour each way and it affects his nerves.'

'But where would we go?'

'Probably Holcombe Brook, so you can still travel to school...'

'Where's that?'

'It's near Ramsbottom.'

I'd been to Accrington a few times with Father and, as we drove through the Rossendale Valley, he'd talked about the towns and villages we passed through. He told me that the Pennine Hills were the millstone grit backbone of England, where the soft waters of the streams and rivers, and the damp air, gave rise to the Industrial Revolution. Some old mills with their tall chimneys were still working in the towns. They were surrounded by terraced, stone houses where the workers lived. There was Ramsbottom, which we thought was funny, although he didn't tell me the locals called it Tupp's Arse, which was even funnier. Haslingden, Rawtenstall and Oswaldtwistle were our favourites. We repeated the words. We rolled them round our tongues, and we laughed. But I didn't remember Holcombe Brook.

'You'll like it. We're going to look at houses there this weekend. You'll have to get used to the idea, Beth, I don't want your father to be ill again.'

We went to view houses; a bungalow on Holcombe Hill was too small and too remote. A Victorian semi on Bolton Road was too big and on the main road. Then they came across plans for a row of terraced houses that were being built. Mother had grown up in the back streets of industrial Salford, the fifth in a family of seven children. A battle with dirt was fought every day by the women of her family. She had always wanted a brand-new house with no Victorian mouldings for dust to settle and where she could have a fitted kitchen. They found what she wanted in the end house of this terrace. It was a redbrick square box on the corner of a road of semis which led down towards fields and on to Bury. It would be ready in August.

'We're not taking any rubbish with us,' said Mother. 'We'll have to get rid of stuff.'

That meant my old toys that I no longer played with. I wished I could take them with me, but the new house was smaller, and my bedroom was the smallest room of all. Mother said I could have a grown-up dressing table to compensate and she couldn't see why I wanted to hang on to things I no longer played with. I looked longingly at my doll's house with its little electric light bulbs, my wind-up musical box that played 'What Shall We Do With The Drunken Sailor?' and my doll's cot with its crocheted blanket; all these had to go. There were piles of *Sunny Stories* and *The Children's Newspaper*, which went in the dustbin. Two dolls and a small teddy which lived on the windowsill were given away. My bigger teddy I hung on to. He sat on a child-size, antique rocking chair that Father had picked up from one of his customers. I still have this chair and teddy bear today. I could keep my books and the wooden bookcase Father had made.

The day we left, I wandered around the house as the removal men staggered about carrying furniture. I had a last look at my bedroom. The murky cream wallpaper was full of scuffs and marks, and there were cut-out pandas stuck on at eye level. I climbed onto the windowsill and looked down into next door's garden. If my friend Joy was there, I would shout down to her. She was often there laughing and having fun with her brothers and sisters. I looked at the tall trees of the wood beyond the garden where Joy and I played, climbing trees and making dens among the rhododendrons and elderflower bushes. I would miss Joy. Tears welled up and rolled down my cheeks. I was leaving so much behind.

'The car's loaded up,' called Father.

'Coming,' I sniffed.

'You'll have to have the cat basket on your knee,' said Father as I came down the stairs.

I walked down the path with Mother, and we stood at the gate looking back at the old house. I lingered, loath to leave.

'Come on,' said Mother. 'Don't forget Jinxy.'

The cat basket containing Jinx our Siamese cat was on the wall next to the gate. As I picked it up, I blinked away more tears.

'I would never forget Jinxy.' I sniffed and got in the car.

Jinx wailed all the way to Holcombe Brook, as if we were murdering her.

Chapter 4
Changes 1958

By the time I started school in September we had settled into our new house. I now had a long walk to the first bus stop, then I had to catch another bus from Bolton town centre to school. I missed walking home with my school friend Janet, and the long chats we used to have. My new bedroom was a tiny, stark white box-room. We couldn't put wallpaper on the walls until the house had dried out, Father said, and that could take up to a year. My room was freezing cold as it had two outside walls, and no heating apart from a two-bar electric fire for winter mornings. My brother John had a bigger room even though he was hardly ever at home. But Mother was happy with her new fitted kitchen, which was clean and modern, and Father seemed pleased that he didn't have to spend so much time travelling.

It was raining as I walked home from the bus that first day back. I'd forgotten my umbrella and my thin gabardine mac was soaked. My satchel was heavy with the books I needed for homework. It seemed to take forever to reach the corner of our road. I was relieved to see our house. I had a key, so I let myself in. The plain-walled house felt empty and cold. I shivered as I took off my coat and went into the kitchen which housed the Aga. Jinx was lying on her piece of old blanket behind the hot plates. That was her favourite place. My father filled up the Aga with anthracite every morning and evening, and Jinx had to be lifted off for this and when Mother was cooking, but she jumped back up again whenever she had the chance. Now she stretched and yawned when she saw me, letting out a little meow. There was a good smell of something cooking; Mother must have put a stew in the oven.

'Where is she, Jinxy?' I said.

Jinx rolled over and I stroked her tummy. She purred. I

wandered into the dining room where a fire was laid. Kneeling, I struck a match, lit the scrunched-up newspaper and watched the orange flames flicker into life. Jinx followed me and we sat together on the rug enjoying the small excitement as the wood caught and the coal started to glow. I fed it from time to time with strategically placed pieces of coal. When the fire seemed to be going well, I wandered back into the kitchen to wash my hands. The sky was dark grey now, the day was closing down, and Mother was late. As I dried my hands, I heard the key in the lock. I went into the cold hall to meet her.

'It's horrible out there,' she said.

'I wondered where you were.'

'Go and put the kettle on, I'll be there in a minute.'

I made a pot of tea and we both sat at the Formica table next to the Aga. She put her elbows on the table and her head in her hands as we waited for the tea to brew. I looked at her greying head of hair. Mother was small and dark. Dumpy, Aunty Elsie had called her. Petite, Father said. I poured the milk into the cups.

'I've been to the doctors,' she said and took a sip of her tea. 'And, well… the thing is I've got to go into hospital, for an operation. Well, it's not really an operation, it's… a procedure. It's nothing really; I mean… having a little lump removed is nothing. I've got a lump here.' She touched her left breast. 'It's a cyst but it's better out.'

Mother's mouth looked wobbly, as if she might cry. I'd never seen her cry. I didn't know what to say or do and I felt as if I might cry myself, but I didn't want to because that might set her off. I looked down at Jinx who was sitting next to us on the floor, and blinked away tears. I stared at the grey and yellow linoleum floor tiles Father had put down; there were a few remnants of the sticky, black stuff that he had stuck them down with still left on their edges. Mother had complained about it getting everywhere. Jinx jumped up onto Mother's knee.

'I'll have to go into hospital next week, it has to be done

23

soon.' She stroked Jinx, pulling the cat's ears down with each stroke. 'I should have gone... anyway, it needs to be done.'

Jinx jumped down; she didn't like having her ears flattened. Mother stood up.

'I'd better put some potatoes on; your father will be here soon. Go and watch the television if you want, I'll call you when tea's ready.'

I did as I was told because I didn't know what else to do. I turned the television on and off. I didn't want to watch the news. I started to do my trigonometry homework. Cold boiled ham, I said to myself, cosine equals base over hypotenuse. But I couldn't concentrate so I just sat there with my books open. Mother had never been ill before. I knew she had had an operation when I was born. It was called a caesarean and it had taken her a long time to recover. This procedure wasn't a proper operation like that; it was only a small thing. But I sensed that something was wrong and that she was trying to pretend everything was all right. I heard the back door slam shut—my father arriving home—and I heard the low hum of their voices through the closed kitchen door. I packed away my maths books and went into the dining room.

I stroked Jinx, who was stretched out in front of the blazing fire. I picked her up; she was limp and sozzled with heat. She allowed herself to be draped around my shoulders and neck, all warm and soft. We sat like that for a few minutes and I watched the fire. I knew Mother was telling Father what she had told me. It was very quiet. I could only catch the occasional murmur. Then the serving hatch from the kitchen opened and Mother popped her head through.

'Tea's ready,' she said. Her voice was pretend cheerful and the false bright look on her face poking through the serving hatch seemed both sad and hilarious. She had had this serving hatch specially made and she was very proud of it. I could feel a hysterical giggle bubbling up inside me. I was frantic to stop it, so I bent over and fussed about removing Jinx from my neck. Father came into the dining room.

'How was school?' he said as he sat at the table. He touched me on the shoulder as he passed me.

'Okay, except the gooseberry crumble was so vile I said I'd be sick if I ate it, the smell of it made me feel ill.'

'I thought it might be better in the senior dining room,' said Mother as she passed the plates of food through the hatch to me.

The three of us started on our beef stew and mashed potatoes. After a few mouthfuls, Father paused.

'What homework have you got tonight?' said Father.

'I've got to learn some French verbs,' I said.

'I'll test you if you like after tea.'

'I've opened a tin of mandarin oranges for afters,' said Mother as she cleared away our plates.

When we'd finished eating, Mother went into the kitchen to wash up. I asked Father if he would test me. He put down his book and smiled at me; he often gave me very loving smiles which I used to enjoy but which more recently I was beginning to feel embarrassed by. I noticed that he had his hand on his side. This was nothing unusual. For as long as I can remember Father had had a pain in his side. He'd had it investigated—barium meals and an investigative operation. All revealed nothing physically wrong with him. It was his nerves, the doctor said. This was the reason he had sold his business in Bolton. But as I think more about this and write about it from my adult view, I wonder why he then bought another business, which he knew nothing about, and which would soon bring him as much stress as the previous business had. As a child I accepted the grown-ups' decisions on this and never even questioned it until now. But surely it wasn't a sensible way forward?

'Beth,' he said. 'Before I test you... I know Mummy has told you that she's going to have a little minor operation done next week—I'm going to get in touch with Aunty Lizzy tomorrow to see if you can go and stay with her while

Mummy is in hospital. Would you like that?'

'Can't I stay here? I want to be near Mummy.'

'We think it's best if you go to Aunty Lizzy's. It should only be for a week or so. Jinx can go with you, Lizzy likes Jinx.'

'Can I take my bicycle?'

'Of course.'

'I could ride to school with Janet like I used to before.'

He smiled a half smile tinged with sadness. I felt sad too. I had never been separated from my mother, apart from the odd night or two when I'd stayed with my aunts, and I wanted to stay at home where I imagined I wouldn't miss her quite so much. But it was just for a few nights and Jinx could go with me.

Father took me to Aunty Lizzy's at the weekend. Aunt Lizzy lived not far from our old house. John called her 'the maiden aunt' because she had never married, and had looked after Grandad until he died the previous year. Grandad had been a bit mad before he died, getting things muddled up and farting when he walked. He didn't do much, just sat in his armchair and read his newspaper while Aunty Lizzy waited on him hand and foot. He never took any notice of me, although for a few months before he died, he came regularly to our house to be looked after by my mother while Aunty Lizzy went to work. They shared him out between the relatives because he kept wandering off and getting lost when he was left alone. He pointed to a pair of my navy-blue, school knickers on the washing line and said, 'That's the boss's top hat.' I told my friend Janet and we laughed at this, pointing to each other's navy-blue knickers as we got changed for gym, repeating the phrase to each other—'That's the boss's top hat'. That's the only thing I can remember him saying to me.

I slept in his old bedroom during my stay with Aunty Lizzy. It had been decorated since he'd died, and the wallpaper had big pink roses all over it. It was much bigger than my box room and I liked the wallpaper. I noticed there was a photograph hanging above the little fireplace. The gold frame looked familiar. I stared at the old photograph—I knew I'd seen it before, but I couldn't think where. It looked so old-fashioned with its faded sepia tones and the ornate frame. The woman wore a dark-coloured dress and a brooch at the high neck with a tiny safety chain attached to it. She had a little smile on her face. There was a definite resemblance to Aunt Lizzy. I studied the photograph, taking in the details and trying to remember where I'd seen it previously.

I couldn't sleep when I went to bed. Where had I seen the photograph before? When was Mother's procedure? Was it the next day? Would she be all right? When would I know? I must ask Aunty Lizzy… I woke up early with the photograph in my mind and I knew where I had seen it before: hanging above the china cabinet in Great-aunt Annie's house.

As I ate my boiled egg, I asked Aunty Lizzy about the photograph.

'I think I saw it at Great-aunt Annie's house,' I said.

'Yes, it's her mother,' she said. I opened my mouth to ask a question but shut it when Aunty Lizzy said, 'Now, hurry up with your breakfast or you'll be late for school.'

From Aunty Lizzy's, I wobbled along the cobbles every morning on my bike to Janet's house. Together we rode along a narrow street between tall, dark cotton mills on our way to school, and thankfully the road surface was smooth. Large wicker baskets full of bales of cotton were always being loaded and unloaded, pulled up and down on pulleys as we swooshed past down the hill, our navy-blue uniform pinafores and maroon blazers flying out behind us, our berets pulled down on our heads so they wouldn't fly off. Whenever the great mill doors opened, we were enveloped in a draught of warm air with fluffy clumps of cotton flying around in it. The rhythmic sound of the massive machines, working looms weaving cotton, shuttles flying, was almost deafening. Women workers who came out of those doors had their hair tied up in scarves with a knot in front on top of their heads. The strands of their hair that escaped had wisps of cotton clinging to them. In the weaving shed they had to learn to lip read as the noise of the machines was so loud, they couldn't hear each other speak. We used to mimic these women mouthing things to each other in an exaggerated way and pointing down between our legs mouthing, 'She's had it all taken away, our Ethel, down below.' We knew we were lucky; we wouldn't be working in a cotton mill. For one thing the cotton trade in Lancashire was dying—these last few working mills had not many years before they were either abandoned and left empty to fall into decay or redeveloped as retail outlets, which were not very successful on the whole. What could you do with these massive buildings? Later still they were marketed as 'loft apartments' which were more popular. In any case, we knew we were destined for better things; we were at the Grammar School, and we had the chance of an education to take us away from that working class existence, to better ourselves.

Janet's mother invited me to stay at the weekend. She asked me how Mother was and all I could say was, 'I don't know, I haven't heard.' My unspoken feelings about Mother came to the surface and I began to sniffle. Janet's mother put her arms round me. She smelled of perfume and cigarettes.

'I'm sure she's fine, Beth,' she said patting my back as I snivelled and sniffed. 'I expect your father's been busy with visiting her and going to work. I'm sure she's fine.'

Aunty Lizzy didn't have a telephone in her house, but the corner shop had one and would take a message if it was important. There hadn't been any messages that I knew of. Aunty Lizzy hadn't said a word about Mother. I worried that something dreadful had happened, that the 'procedure' had not proceeded as it should, or that my mother had died, and they thought I would be better off not knowing. Surely, they'd have to tell me some time. I didn't really believe this had happened, but I couldn't bring myself to ask. I was too worried and frightened. If I didn't ask, I could hope that everything was well. I realise through writing about this how undeveloped my language for feelings was. No one ever asked me how I felt, and I don't remember anyone talking about how they felt; my parents and their families certainly didn't. Much later in life when I was a nurse tutor, and when the NHS would still pay for such things, I did a two year part-time experiential training course for use with student nurses, and at a personal level I think that was where I began to learn to talk about my feelings—that and at Rochdale Marriage Guidance Council (now Relate), where I started my part-time training as a marriage guidance counsellor around the same time.

Later that week I was staying with Aunty Lizzy, she answered the doorbell one evening and I could hear her talking to someone. She shouted through to me: 'Beth, I'm going to the shop to make a phone call, I won't be long.'

I had finished my homework and was sitting next to the fire with Jinx on my knee. I stroked her and thought about the phone call. Did this mean bad news? Was Mother all right? Or not? I buried my face in the cat's soft fur. My insides clenched and knotted. I felt sick.

'Jinxy-pooh,' I said. 'Do you want to go home?'

Jinx purred extra loud, a rolling lushness of a purr to let me know she knew how I was feeling. I picked up the *Radio Times* to see if there was anything on the television, but it was Armand and Michaela Denis on safari in Africa. I used to watch it with John when he was home, and we laughed about Armand's strong French accent, which we loved to mimic. Now, John was living in London and training to be a bank manager, so I didn't see him often. I didn't feel like watching Armand and Michaela without John to laugh with, so I sat next to the little bookshelf and took down one of Aunty Lizzy's books about the Royal Family. Aunty Lizzy was proud of having the same name as the Queen. This book had pictures of the Queen when she was Princess Elizabeth, and there was a picture of her all dressed in black with a veil over her face when she was at her father's funeral.

Just then Aunty Lizzy came back.

'That was your father on the phone. He says to tell you that your mother has had her operation.'

'An operation?' So, she was alive.

'Yes, they've had to take a bit more away, the lump had spread a bit,' she said. Aunty Lizzy made a sort of circling motion with her hand round her left breast.

'Oh no,' I said, wondering what all this meant. 'So, is she… is she, all right?'

'Yes, she will be, it was just a bigger thing than they thought,' said Aunty Lizzy. 'Anyway, your father's coming on Saturday to take you to see her.'

'Oh good,' I said. 'I'd like to see her. Where is she? Is she still in hospital?'

'Yes.'

'When will she go home?'

'What a lot of questions,' said Aunty Lizzy and went into the kitchen.

Father came on Saturday afternoon. I was all ready to go, wearing my blue jacket and grey skirt. I knew Mother liked me in this outfit. As we drove along, Father said, 'Aunty Lizzy told you, didn't she, about Mummy?'

'About the procedure becoming an operation?'

'Yes, what they do is… they take out a piece of the lump and send it to the laboratory and then, if necessary, they take away some more, and that's what they had to do for your mother, they took away more of the surrounding tissue.' He sighed. 'And, well… they… they actually… removed her breast, Beth. It's called a mastectomy.'

'A mastectomy?' I repeated trying to take it in. His voice had become so quiet that I could hardly hear what he said. I shuddered. Removing a breast sounded very serious and painful.

'Yes,' he said. 'That's right. So, she's not fully recovered yet, she's still in hospital and will be for another week or two, I think.' He was speaking carefully and slowly as if he was thinking about each word. He was always a bit like that,

Father, but this was more than usual. 'By the way, in case you're wondering where we're going... Mummy's in a different hospital now. She didn't like it in Bury General, so... Dr Kelly and I brought her home and then... well, anyway, we took her to Rochdale, to Birch Hill Hospital. She's got a private room there. It's better for her.'

Something was very wrong. I couldn't speak. If I spoke, I might cry, and I knew Father was sad and upset. I didn't want to upset him more and make him ill.

Birch Hill Hospital was huge. It was an old stone building with a tall tower. Father said it was the old workhouse where poor people with nowhere to live had gone in Victorian times. I wondered how anyone ever found their way around somewhere so massive. We walked along miles of corridors and up several flights of stairs. Mother must be in the tower. There was a strong smell of chloroform. I'd had my tonsils out when I was six and I'd never forgotten that hospital smell. It was a wonder everyone didn't pass out after they'd been in Birch Hill Hospital for a while.

Mother's room was small. There was just enough space for Father and me on either side of the bed. Mother was propped up against a pile of pillows, looking pale. There was a bottle hanging on a stand with a tube leading from it which went into her arm, and her whole chest was completely bandaged up with another tube coming out from under her arm. It was draining rusty coloured fluid into a bag and the bandage round her chest had a dark red stain on it. She opened her eyes when we came in, but she seemed groggy and she didn't smile at us or speak. Father sat on the only chair and took hold of her hand. Then suddenly she coughed, moaned and clutched at her chest with the hand that was attached to the tube. She coughed again and Father found a little metal bowl to hold under her chin. She coughed and groaned then half spat, and half vomited up green stuff into the bowl. She lay back exhausted and closed her eyes. Father looked at me.

'I don't think we should stay long.'

I nodded and looked down. I concentrated on watching the fluid drip-drip in a little chamber part way along the tube. Mother fell asleep. Father stood up and pointed at the door. Out in the corridor, a nurse smiled at us.

'She was sick, so we've left her to rest,' he said.

The nurse nodded. 'She's just had something for her pain, that can make her sick.'

'I'll be back later; will you tell her?'

We walked in silence through the miles of hospital corridors. I was glad I'd seen Mother, but she looked very ill. I couldn't get that image out of my head of her lying in bed with tubes and bloody bandages everywhere. It kept coming back to me even though I tried hard to think of happier times, like when she couldn't stop laughing at something last Christmas, or when she was walking around the garden on a sunny day showing me the roses and telling me their names.

It was to be a few weeks before I saw Mother again. I went to the corner shop with Aunty Lizzy every Wednesday evening to speak to Father on the telephone. Aunty Lizzy told me not to mither him about going to see Mother as he had enough to do without driving backwards and forwards to take me to see her. My anxieties about Mother and my fear of her dying lessened as time went by, and each week Father reassured me that she was improving. It must have been only a matter of a month or so before I went home as it was the weekend before half-term when Father collected me and Jinx from Aunt Lizzy's. It had seemed like several months to me.

'Your Mother will be pleased to see you,' he said as we drove home. 'But she's not completely well yet, and you and John will have to help her this week.'

'Is John coming home?'

'Yes, for a week or so.'

'Goody, goody,' I said. Life was much more fun when

John was around.

'Mummy has been very poorly,' said Father. 'It all turned out to be more... complicated than we thought. As well as the operation—we don't know why it happened—she had a sort of breakdown.'

'What does that mean?'

'Well, what happened, when she was in Bury General... it was probably the drugs for the pain or the shock of the... the bigger operation... anyway she was imagining things, and... it was very disturbing for her, well... for everyone in fact. Now she needs to rest, and you must be very good and not upset her.' His voice was serious and quiet.

'What was she imagining?'

'Oh, all sorts of things... things that weren't there, anyway she wouldn't stay in Bury General, that's why we took her to Birch Hill Hospital.' There was a small silence. 'Anyway, she's much better but these things take time, we'll all have to help.' He glanced at me. His eyes and face were sad.

'She'll be pleased to see John,' I said.

'Yes,' said Father, his mouth set in a straight line.

Mother said John and Father didn't get on because of the War. Father was called up to join the army when John was three and was away from home for six years. Mother kept the business running during that time and employed a housekeeper to look after John. When Father returned, John clung to Mother's skirts and said, 'Who's that man? I don't like him.' Then they had me and Father made me his favourite. Mother always said I could wind him round my little finger. But I knew John was her favourite.

Mother was sitting in the lounge when we arrived. The coal fire made the room feel warm and cosy. I opened Jinx's travelling basket, and after a sniff and a cautious look around, she wandered over to the fire and began to wash herself. We all watched her.

'She's made herself at home straight away,' said Mother. 'Beth, I'm sure you've grown.'

John came into the lounge. 'Betty,' he said and came over to me and tried to tickle me on my stomach. I giggled and fended him off. He always called me 'Betty' to tease me because he knew I didn't like it.

'What's this?' he said leaning over and pointing at Mother's chest. She laughed.

'You cheeky monkey,' she said. 'It's my falsie, it's not very good, it keeps riding up, I'm forever pushing it down, I'll have to get a better one.'

I hadn't thought about her having to wear a falsie. It didn't look right; it was nothing like her real breast on the other side of her chest. I sat down next to her.

'I'm glad you're back,' I said.

'Yes,' said Mother. She put her arm round my shoulder. 'So am I.'

Mother was tired and needed to rest in the afternoons. Her arm on the side where she had had the operation was painful and difficult to move. They'd had to remove the lymph glands, she said, and that meant fluid accumulated in her arm. She did exercises to help it. Father went to work, and John and I helped with the shopping and housework. We did the washing-up together in the evenings. He teased me and made me laugh by flicking water at me when he washed up, and by sending back pots to be washed again, saying they weren't done properly, when I washed up. He had a great ability to make everything fun. When I saw him, I wished he was at home all the time.

On the Friday, he went back to London. Mother went upstairs for a rest in the afternoon. I sat next to the fire with Jinx for a while. I was working my way through my parents' bookcase. I'd read all my own books and John's, and now I was reading *Love on the Dole*. Father had said it wasn't suitable for me, but nobody had noticed I was reading it. I decided I would finish the chapter first, but remembering I must look after Mother, I thought I'd make a cup of tea for her. I walked up the stairs, carefully balancing the cup of tea on a little tray. Mother's bedroom door was ajar, so I put my head round. The curtains were closed but she wasn't in bed. She was standing naked in front of her long mirror. She didn't try to cover herself when she saw me, she just continued to stand there. Our eyes met in the mirror.

'It's my operation,' she said.

We both looked at the scar in the mirror as her fingers traced the line of it which went from the centre of her chest to under her arm. Her chest seemed to cave in on that side. The scar was jagged and dented in places as if someone had hacked at her chest gouging out the flesh. It didn't look surgical. It was livid red, blue and grey.

'It'll go better with time, like this,' she said.

Her fingers moved to touch the scar which went down the middle of her stomach. It had faded with time, but the scar tissue in the middle was wide, and her skin was puckered up on each side of it. We both gazed at her butchered body. It was a shocking sight and I was unable to speak. She'd had the caesarean because the afterbirth was blocking my way out of her womb. It had saved both our lives. I felt a flicker of responsibility even though the doctor had said it was just one of those things; it could happen to anyone.

Chapter 5
Britannia Street 1881

I'm searching both for my ancestors and for a part of myself that I've locked away and not wanted to see before. That's why I've left it so long. It might be a painful and difficult journey and I'm thinking about having therapy. But finding a therapist is not simple. I know all the local therapists and they know me. I ask around my psychotherapy contacts for people further afield. There must be no previous connection between the therapist and me. We must start with a clean slate. The therapist needs to form their own independent opinion of me, and me of him or her. I'm recommended a man who has recently moved into the next town from London. His name is James and he's psychoanalytically trained like me. Do I want a man? My previous therapists have always been women. I usually feel at ease with women, but it could be useful to move out of my comfort zone. He may have a different view, a male view, whatever that might mean. I decide to go and see him for a preliminary meeting. The drive isn't too bad, about half an hour, and my first impressions are good. He's younger than me, in his forties, and he seems kind and thoughtful. We meet a couple of times before a decision is made. I tell him of my compelling need to research my family, and of my obsession with my teenage years. He comments that these two periods of time may have some connection that holds some meaning for me. I agree. But when I return home and think more about it, I feel that this is a journey I must make alone. I want to explore this story myself. I go to meet James for a third time and tell him of my decision. We agree that I can always contact him again if I feel differently at any time.

I tell my grown-up daughters about this family history research. About the secrets and the lies of omission. How strange, they remark, that so much shame was attached to illegitimacy in the past, when nowadays it is seen as normal that people live together and have children without marrying. I still find it difficult to talk about my past. I have never talked about it to my children and many of my friends know very little about that time. Alicia, my eldest daughter, is the one most interested in the family history research, particularly as she has lived in and around Lancaster since 1989 when she moved there with her young daughter, Chloe. And she is the only one who remembers my mother and my brother, John. They all remember my father as a sick old man. Rebecca was four when he died, Miranda seven and Alicia thirteen.

Alicia lives in Halton, a village just outside Lancaster. We're both interested in this coincidence, that she lives near Lancaster where my father's family came from. We talk about the evidence we already have, and I refer to Grandad's birth certificate. Does she know Britannia Street, where Great-grandmother Elizabeth Cock gave birth to Albert Edward, my grandfather? Alicia can't find it in the Lancaster A–Z. She will investigate.

I trawl the Internet for family history sites, and sign up for www.ancestry.co.uk, which has an offer—free use of the website for a fortnight. I go to the website, click on search, and fill in the details from Grandad's birth certificate. Details of birth, marriage and death records come up, as well as census records. I go to the 1881 census. It's the one nearest Grandad's birth so perhaps Elizabeth and Albert will still be in Britannia Street. Click. There is Britannia Street. It's simple. Click and I am taken from twenty-first-century Manchester to nineteenth-century Lancaster. There is 1881 before me in the form of a scanned copy of the original census document. The perfect copperplate handwriting is stunning, a work of art. What care has been taken to write down the details of the families who lived at numbers 4, 5, 6, 7 and 8, Britannia Street, in the Ecclesiastical Parish of St Thomas's, the Municipal Ward of Queen's, in the Township of Lancaster. What a long, laborious task it must have been. Whoever wrote it, probably a man, has literally left his mark on these pages. Now it can be seen anywhere in the world, conjured up by a magic click. I am taken aback by the strength of feeling I experience as I study this writing on the screen. I'm emotional, moved to see before me the lives of the people who were born, lived, worked and died in Victorian Lancaster. What would these Victorians, the people of Britannia Street, make of this digital age?

The listing of the occupants of Britannia Street shows that these were working people. They were cotton weavers, joiners, general labourers, dressmakers, milliners' apprentices, everyone described by their relation to the head of the household. In number 8 lives the Cock family. The head of the household is Esther Cock, aged fifty-four, a widow whose occupation is listed as housekeeper. Beneath Esther is Elizabeth, her daughter aged twenty-eight—my great-grandmother. Her occupation was domestic servant. Esther is therefore my great-great-grandmother. Then there are Elizabeth's brothers and sisters. Christopher is aged twenty-two, his occupation is listed as compositor. Is that a job he did in a cotton mill? Then another Esther, a daughter aged twenty, a cotton weaver. William, aged eighteen, is a plasterer, and last of all is Albert Edward, described as grandson. He is Esther's grandson, Elizabeth's son and my grandfather. He is five years old and a scholar.

I have found Albert Edward and Elizabeth, and her family. She is not alone as I imagined. She has a mother, two brothers and a sister. They have not thrown her out at all. In fact, it looks as if just the opposite happened, that she remained with her family and that her mother looked after the home for all her grown-up children while they worked and little Albert went to school. Now I'm so happy that Elizabeth was not on her own, so pleased that they did not abandon her. They look to be thriving, all of them are working. They must have had money coming in. They were all born in Lancaster, except Esther their mother, whose place of birth was Ingleton, in the West Riding of Yorkshire, a place close to the Lancashire border.

I wonder about the consecutive numbering of the houses. There seem to be houses on one side of the street only. Alicia telephones, she has found the answer in the Lancaster archives where they have old maps. One of these maps has been photographed, enlarged and put up on the wall in the Lancaster museum where the archives are kept. By coincidence, Britannia Street is on this map. Alicia spoke with the curator who told her that Britannia Street was one of a series of courtyards and alleyways near the canal in the centre of Lancaster. This type of housing built around a courtyard was built for the workers that the cotton industry enticed into the city in the second half of the eighteenth century, when Lancaster was a busy port. The curator said the housing was poor quality, built cheaply and badly. These courts and alleyways became notorious for their poor living standards, which was thought to contribute to drunkenness and debauchery. Running water would only have been available from a standpipe in the courtyard. The sanitation was primitive, a row of privies in the courtyard serving several families.

I'm intrigued by the street name. Britannia is the national female personification of the United Kingdom. She pre-dates Roman times and has developed over the centuries to become the warrior, goddess figure we know today from the image on our 50p coins. She carries a trident and a shield with the union flag on it. She is an emblem of maritime power and unity. 'Rule Britannia' is a stirring tune that fosters patriotism. Was the street named with all this in mind? To encourage the workers to bear their hardships and their struggles in the spirit of striving for the greater good of the country? Whatever the case, the housing was not well built, and it was demolished in the 1920s. The area was cleared. In the 1970s a small block of flats was built on the site overlooking the now picturesque canal. But in 1881 Britannia Street was a slum.

Their lives would have been hard, and I am moved—saddened. These long dead ancestors are living in my head and I visualise the courtyard of Britannia Street with its row of privies in the middle. Washing is strung on lines across the yard and stinking puddles of water lie in holes in the cobbles near the standpipe which is at one side. How did they come to live here? What happened to Elizabeth's father, Esther's husband, my great-great-grandfather? Will I find any clues as to the identity of Albert's father? Did Elizabeth have more brothers and sisters? What has happened to them all?

I am shocked at the strength of my response. Seeing them and their lives recorded alongside their neighbours brings them sharply into focus as real people. The lives they lived are before my eyes, not just a story passed down the generations, which was not quite accurate, but hard facts, dispassionately written by a clerk in immaculate copperplate handwriting. I find it hard to leave the computer, but I also need time and space between my research sessions. I feel so strongly about what I'm learning that I need time to examine the facts and process the strong emotions generated in me. There are also other calls on my time, such as babysitting my grandchildren. I resolve to buy a laptop so I can research on the move whenever I feel ready to walk down Britannia Street again.

Chapter 6

Down the Railway Line 1958

Back in 1958, the journey from Holcombe Brook to Bolton School involved two bus rides. The first one took about half an hour so there was time to observe the other passengers, and the regulars soon became familiar to me. There were five girls from my school who got on the bus in the mornings. Two of them were in the sixth form and they sat together. Two were the vicar's daughters. These four all boarded the bus before me. The fifth was in the year above me and she got on at the stop after mine. I was fascinated by what this girl had done to her school uniform. Her coat was tied tightly at her waist with a leather belt which was knotted instead of buckled up. Her velour hat was shaped like a cowboy's Stetson, her tie was loosely tied, and her white shirt collar was unbuttoned at the top. What a cool cat. (I'd watched a music programme on television with John called *Cool For Cats*.) She smiled and sat next to me.

'You're Beth Cox, aren't you?'

I nodded.

'I recognise you from that reading competition you won last year. I'm Cathy, Cathy Evans. Have you just moved here?' she said. 'I saw you on the bus before, in September, but then you disappeared.'

'I went to stay with my aunt in Bolton... I only came back at half-term.'

'Where do you live?'

'Just off Longsight Road, near the tennis club,' I said. 'What about you?'

'Greenmount, the next village.'

'I haven't been there,' I said. 'I don't know my way round here.'

'It's easy to get to from where you live, down the railway line.'

41

'I've heard the trains, I thought it was all fenced off.'

'You can get through where the fence is broken. I'll show you if you like—will you be on the half past four bus?'

I nodded. Cathy told me about her family. She was the youngest of four. Her eldest brother, Russell, was a Don at Oxford University, her sister Tessa worked in their father's chemist's shop in the next village, the other brother was Gareth, and he was doing his A levels. He'd already been offered a place at Oxford.

At school the first lesson was geography. We were studying Ordnance Survey maps and my mind wandered onto the railway line. I knew a bit about it as Mother had said it was a shame it had closed as a passenger service a year or two before we moved. It started at Holcombe Brook, went to Greenmount, then on to Manchester with several more stations along the way. Now a steam train chuffed its way up and down the line once or twice a day with no stops. I never did discover why it went up and down the line. As far as I can remember it had a few trucks attached to the engine sometimes, but other times it was just an engine. You could hear its hooter from our house. When I got off the bus, I walked past the station yard every day. The iron gates were padlocked, and the yard was full of old wagons. Nothing much seemed to happen there.

That afternoon travelling back with Cathy, I was quickly aware that I was not 'with it'. Cathy was very 'with it'. She didn't read comics like *Girl*, which I read and which was full of pictures of ballet dancers, Alicia Markova and Margot Fonteyn, and had strip cartoons called 'Lettice Leafe' and 'Belle Of The Ballet' in it. Cathy had a magazine of her sister's with her which had pictures of James Dean and Elvis Presley in it, and tips about make-up and hairstyles. Cathy told me that her brother Gareth had recorded music from the radio and wired up their house so they could have pop music playing through speakers all over the house whenever they wanted.

'Where do you record the music from?' I asked. My

father had bought a tape recorder, a new thing only recently available, to practise his French pronunciation with. Perhaps I could use it to record music.

'Radio Luxembourg, it's on late at night,' she said.

Back home, I looked in the *Radio Times* to find Radio Luxembourg. There it was. Every night after that, I took the radio up from the kitchen when I went to bed, tuned in to Radio Luxembourg and played it very quietly so I wouldn't disturb anyone. It played all the latest pop music, much of it American: Elvis Presley, Gene Vincent and Brenda Lee. I had never heard anything like it. The rawness, the no-holds-barredness, the sexiness of it; I loved it all. The music I had grown up with was my parents playing the piano. Mother played the classics, Beethoven and Chopin, and Father played hymns by ear. 'The Lord's My Shepherd I'll Not Want' was his favourite. John had a record player, but he was into modern jazz, which I wasn't keen on. I had two singles, Tommy Steele, 'Singing The Blues', and Paul Anka, 'Diana', which I had bought with my pocket money. I played those records repeatedly crouched next to John's record player, listening and singing along.

Cathy and I got off the bus at the Hare and Hounds pub and crossed the road to the old station. We peered through the gates into the goods yard. Paint was peeling off the wooden carriages lined up in the yard, the wheels were rusted and rosebay willowherb grew everywhere. Cathy rattled the gates. They didn't budge. A notice read *Trespassers will be Prosecuted*.

'How do we get in?' I said.

'There are loads of places,' said Cathy. 'I'll show you.'

'Won't we get into trouble?'

Cathy laughed. 'Course not, no one will know and anyway everyone uses it as a short cut.'

'What about the trains?'

'They're only once or twice a day, you just have to listen out for them.' We walked down Longsight Road and Cathy turned up the first avenue. 'It's up here.'

At the end of the avenue was a broken wooden fence. We climbed through under the brambles. I felt guilty and looked around to see if anyone was watching. We walked across an overgrown bank of weeds and grass with a few spindly shrubs dotted around. Here was the single-track railway line. It was bordered on both sides by rough grass and weeds, with fields on the right-hand side beyond a low hedge. On the left was a high, wild hedge through which I caught glimpses of houses. We walked down the middle of the track, taking big strides to land on the sleepers.

'The track goes all the way past the cul-de-sac where my house is,' said Cathy. 'It's easy to find, it's the first house you come to on the right.'

Cathy showed me where to clamber under another bit of broken fence which brought me out just around the corner from my house. I didn't tell Mother about walking down the railway line.

I arranged to go to Cathy's house one Saturday morning after I'd done my job of going to the shop for bread. I went through the broken fence and walked across the grass. The feeling of entering forbidden territory was one I never managed to fully shift. It was lonely and quiet. I felt vulnerable and guilty. There were trains to watch out for, and other potential dangers for young girls by themselves in lonely places. I stood still for a moment and looked both ways, it was quiet, there was no sign of a train. The track curved round a bend either way so I couldn't see far, but I thought I would hear a train approaching. I stepped over the track onto a sleeper and turned left. I concentrated on walking from sleeper to sleeper between the rails. This rhythmic striding had the effect of calming me down as I progressed down the line. It took about ten minutes to reach Hillview Avenue. I could walk straight onto the unpaved cul-de-sac where Cathy's house was. There were no fences or brambles to stop me and there was Cathy's house just as she had described. When Cathy opened the door, two dogs rushed at me.

'Don't touch Jack, the little one,' said Cathy as I bent down to stroke them. 'He's a bit bad-tempered until he gets to know you.'

She took me through the square hall and into the front room.

'I'll get Gareth to put the music on for us,' said Cathy. 'Do you want a coffee?'

'Yes please.'

I sat on the battered, brown velvet sofa which had dog hairs on it and looked round. There was an upright piano behind the sofa, and a desk and chair in one corner. The wallpaper was dull cream with bunches of faded peach flowers scattered across it. It looked old-fashioned and there were marks and scuffs here and there on it. It felt homely though and I didn't mind the dog hairs. It meant they were relaxed about the house, something my mother was not. Cathy came back with three mugs of coffee and a sugar bowl on a tray. A boy followed her in. Immediately I thought of some lines from *Twelfth Night*, which we'd been studying at school. *Not yet old enough for a man, nor young enough for a boy.* That described him perfectly. He was older and taller than Cathy, slightly built and with the same intelligent-looking, grey eyes and thick brown hair. He was good-looking. He wore grey flannel trousers and a shirt. Cathy had some tight jeans on with a sloppy-joe sweater. I wanted some tight jeans, but Mother said I didn't need them. I had my grey skirt on. The music was playing through a speaker near the door.

'Gareth's recorded it for us,' said Cathy. 'It's Little Richard.'

'I can't stay long; I've got to get back to swotting,' said Gareth as he plugged in a two-bar electric fire and sat down on the rug. Cathy sat next to me on the sofa. I had never heard Little Richard before. He plonked and banged away on the piano faster and louder than anyone I had ever heard. He screamed and shouted '*Lucille!*'. I had never heard anything like it. It was raucous, primitive. I was overwhelmed by the sheer, forbidden sexiness of it, blood suffused my face.

'He's mad, you know, he's been in a loony bin,' said Gareth.

'He sounds a bit mad,' I said.

'Yeah, but he's good,' said Cathy.

'He puts his leg up on the piano and plays standing up, his hands under his leg,' said Gareth. 'Like this.' He got up and demonstrated at the piano. Cathy and I laughed. Gareth was funny, uninhibited. My face reddened further. It must be puce by now.

'Do you like Elvis?' Gareth asked me.

I nodded, feeling shy because I didn't really know, but keen to give the right answer.

'Cool,' he said. 'So, do we. He'll be on in a minute.' He nodded towards the speaker.

The door opened and a woman poked her head round. She had the same eyes and slim build as Cathy and Gareth. She came into the room with a cigarette in her hand.

'Hello,' she said to me, smiling. 'Is this Beth?'

'Yes,' I said. 'Hello.'

'Nice to meet you,' she said. 'Cathy told me about you.' She turned to Gareth and Cathy. 'I'm going into town now to the market; I'll be a couple of hours.'

'Okay,' said Cathy. 'We might go to Roz's.'

'Haven't you work to do, Gareth?' said Mrs Evans.

'Yeah, I'm just having a quick break,' said Gareth raising his cup of coffee up. With a nod, Mrs Evans left.

'Who's Roz?' I said.

'Roz Ashworth, she lives at the other end of the avenue. We went to Greenmount Primary together, but she goes to Bury Grammar now,' Cathy said.

Gareth got up. 'I'd better get on,' he said. 'See you around.' He shut the door behind him.

'He's going to Oxford,' said Cathy. 'So, he's got to get good results.'

'He must be very clever,' I said.

'He is,' she said. 'He's not seventeen until next year, but they moved him up a class so he's doing everything early.'

We finished our coffee and went to find Roz. We walked past the two big detached houses with gardens and lawns in front that separated Cathy and Roz's houses. Roz's was the fourth house on Hillview Avenue, the first if you came by the main road. The one next to Roz's had three cars parked on its drive, in front of a double garage. One was a sports car, another a large Jaguar and the third was a funny-looking car like a tin can on its side and on wheels.

'The people who live here are an old couple,' said Cathy pointing to the house next to hers. 'We hardly ever see them. But the Browns, well, there's always a lot going on there.' She laughed and pointed to the strange car. 'That's Adrian's hot rod, he gives Roz and me rides up and down the avenue in it.'

The curtains were closed at Roz's house. Cathy rang the bell. No one came for a while. I looked at my watch; it was half-past eleven.

'Do you think they're still in bed?' I said.

'I'm sure Roz'll be down in a minute,' said Cathy.

Roz's face appeared at the glass panel in the front door. She disappeared and then unlocked the door. She wore a floaty pyjama top with matching knickers. Her long legs were tanned, and her blonde hair hung over her face. She pushed it behind her ears.

'Hi, come on in.' She grinned at us. There was something friendly and easy about her. I warmed to her straight away. We followed her through a small living room dark with closed curtains into the kitchen at the back of the house. The sink and draining board were full of unwashed dishes. Mother would never allow that.

'Coffee?' said Roz.

'Yes please,' I said. Roz rummaged around in the sink and rinsed out three mugs.

'We'll go up to my room,' she said while we waited for

the kettle to boil. 'Be quiet so we don't wake the parents.' She grabbed a packet of chocolate digestives.

Roz's room was tiny, a bit like mine, but the bed was unmade, and clothes and books were in piles on the floor. There were so many things on the floor, and clothes hanging up in a squash behind the door that it wouldn't open properly. Being slim we slipped through the gap, but anyone bigger than us would have had difficulty. A chest of drawers was covered in pieces of jewellery, make-up, and more piles of paper and magazines. It looked like an exotic bazaar to me. We sat on Roz's bed with our mugs and the packet of biscuits. Before she sat down, Roz picked up a scrunched-up garment off the bed and threw it on the floor.

'Are those your new baby-dolls?' said Cathy.

'Oh yes, do you like them?' Roz held up the tiny knickers and waved them in the air. 'Here's the top.' She waved another garment around. So, she had two pairs of these baby-doll pyjamas. I thought about my two nightdresses, which were like Victorian children's nightwear by comparison.

'Those are lovely,' Cathy said. 'Did you get them from Dorothy Perkins in Bury?'

'Yeah, £2 9s 11d. They're cool, aren't they?'

'Show Beth those photographs that Gareth took,' said Cathy.

Roz rummaged around in the piles of stuff on her chest of drawers. She retrieved a handful of photographs and thrust them into my hand. The black-and-white photographs were of Cathy and Roz dressed in their school uniforms but what they had done to those uniforms gave me a shock at first, then it made me laugh. They had hitched up their gym slips so high that you could nearly see their knickers. In fact, I as flicked through the pile of photographs, there was one where you *could* see their knickers. They were bending over with their hockey sticks poised ready to bully off. They had stockings pulled up over their knees, and the flesh at the top of their thighs and their knickers was visible. They had both squashed their hats into the cowboy shape I had first noticed on Cathy. On another photo they had cigarettes between their fingers.

'What do you think?' said Cathy.

'You look as if you've just escaped from St Trinian's,' I said.

They both laughed. 'Gareth likes photography, he develops them himself. Usually he photographs trains...'

Cathy stopped as the door was pushed open as far as it would go and a tousled, bleached-blonde head appeared. I assumed it was Roz's mother. She stood in the doorway and fumbled in her dressing-gown pocket, pulling out a packet of cigarettes.

'Hello girls,' she smiled at us. 'Who's this?'

'It's Beth, from Cathy's school, she's just moved to Holcombe Brook,' said Roz.

'Oh really, whereabouts?' said Mrs Ashworth still fumbling in her pocket. 'I can't find my lighter.'

'Northgate Avenue,' I said.

'That's nice,' said Mrs Ashworth. 'Did you walk down the railway line?'

'Yes.' I nodded.

'Be careful of the trains.'

'Yes, Mother, thank you,' said Roz.

Mrs Ashworth shook her head and disappeared. Roz pulled something out from behind her.

'Look at these,' she said. 'Sorry they're a bit squashed, I must have been sitting on them.'

They were more photographs of Cathy and Roz sitting perched on the back of Adrian's hot rod car dressed in their sexy school uniforms and some close-ups of their faces wearing heavy make-up. We looked through the photos, drank our coffee and ate the chocolate biscuits. Roz brushed her hair and then offered to brush mine, which was tied up in a ponytail. I looked at my watch; it was nearly quarter-past twelve. I wanted to stay longer, but I had to get back for dinner at twelve-thirty.

As I walked back up the railway line, I thought about Hillview Avenue. Both Roz's and Cathy's houses were in the kind of slightly shabby, untidy state that I knew my mother would think of as scruffy and that she would not allow in our house. But I felt relaxed in those houses where it looked as if no one minded if you spilt your drink. They looked to me as if a family lived in them, a family with animals. I had always longed for a bigger family and for more animals. For a while when I was very young, I had begged my mother for a baby brother or sister. John was so much older than me and he wanted to be with his friends, not me. I wasn't sure of many things at that time, but one thing I did know even at that young age was that I was determined to have babies of my own, a few if possible, to make a family. I was very happy when my father brought home two tabby kittens one evening. Finally, some companions to love and care for other than Joy, whose mother often seemed determined to keep me away from her, coming up with excuses as to why she couldn't play with me, which I didn't believe. How many times do you have to tidy your sock drawer? Who has a sock drawer anyway?

Chapter 7
Britannia Street 1891

Everything is in place for my journey, a new laptop is up and running, and a new printer is installed. Whenever I have a chunk of time, and I feel ready, I'm searching through the genealogical websites. I bought a year's membership of Ancestry when the free fortnight expired. I am hooked. I sit at the kitchen table with my coffee and shut everything else out. I'm going back to Victorian Lancaster. I'm excited.

The census was taken every ten years, just as it is now. The first census with people in it was 1841, before that it was just property. Shall I go forward in time from 1881 first or backward? Forward to see what has happened to Elizabeth during those ten years. Click. Click. I'm in nineteenth-century Lancaster: 1891. The original scanned document appears. The magic of the Internet. Like the 1881 form, it is written in beautiful copperplate handwriting, it's like a work of art.

This time the Cock family are first on the page. They are still in Britannia Street. Now Elizabeth, aged thirty-eight is head of the family. She has taken her mother's place as head of the household and housekeeper. Great-great-grandmother Esther must have died. When and how did she die? My grandfather Albert is sixteen and working as a warehouseman. And here now is Annie, Great-aunt Annie, whose table precipitated the sharing of secrets by my parents; she is Elizabeth's second illegitimate child. Annie is six and described as a scholar. How shocking that must have been, a second child ten years after the first and no sign of a husband. Elizabeth's sister Esther, a cotton weaver, now aged thirty, is still living in Britannia Street and so is her brother, William, plasterer and slater, now twenty-eight. Christopher is no longer there. I search for Great-great-grandmother Esther's death. I find the record, she died three years before in 1888. I request a death certificate.

I take a trip online around the streets of nineteenth-century Lancaster. Not far from Britannia Street were three of the institutions that Lancaster was known for. The Lunatic Asylum. The Home for Orphaned and Fatherless Children. The Workhouse. The names alone are terrifying. What must it have been like living in the shadow of these places? Was it their very proximity that caused Elizabeth and her family to decide to look after Grandad Albert and Great-aunt Annie, Elizabeth's two fatherless children? In any case, Elizabeth did not rush to marry. Maybe the fathers of the children were already married, or maybe she did not want to marry. Did they have the same father or two different ones? I really want to know the answers. I wish there was still someone alive who knew her. She must have been a strong woman to bear the brunt of her unmarried status and two illegitimate children. I admire her.

I visit Lancaster regularly to see Alicia, and I am familiar with the centre of the city where Britannia Street was situated. It is a relatively small city and it is almost entirely stone built. The stone castle dominates the city centre. It belongs to the Queen, and, as the monarch, she has inherited the title of Duke of Lancaster. The monarch, whether male or female, inherits the dukedom. Castles with dungeons and fortifications were often used as prisons, and Lancaster Castle was a prison until 2011. It must have been one of the last in the country to be used as a prison. Nowadays you can take a guided tour and see the court room and the cells where prisoners were kept.

There is a great, sprawling stone building that was once a cotton mill, within walking distance of where Britannia Street was situated. Now divided into smaller units, there are businesses of all kinds and restaurants in what were once the massive spaces containing looms and where bales of cotton from the West Indies were stored. Was this where members of the Cock family worked?

Present-day Lancaster has had some of its stonework

cleaned but there are buildings and walls where the stone is as black as it must have been in the 1800s. There are stone-flagged alleyways, and shops with ancient-looking windows above modern shop fronts, and some old cobbled streets remain. If it rains, which it often does, there is a greyness, a melancholy to the place; it's not a pretty city like Chester or York, overrun by tourists. The old institutions have closed, the buildings and land sold to developers, and people are cared for in the community.

Lancaster feels old. It carries the weight of the past—the infamous witch trials of the 1600s, its time as an industrial port, when it was part of the cotton/slave triangle, so called because boats sailed between Africa, the West Indies and Lancashire, transporting goods and slaves. Black slaves were not uncommon in Lancaster. Some were sold on, and others were kept in Lancaster to work in the homes of people who could afford them, and who saw nothing wrong in this. It was a lucrative trade and Lancaster grew wealthy on it. At Sunderland Point near Heysham, in a field on unconsecrated ground (he was not a Christian), is the grave of a young black man who died in 1736. It's known as 'Sambo's grave'.

At that time tall ships set sail for Africa, America the West Indies from the mouth of the River Lune. These ships exported everything that could possibly be needed in the colonies, most of which had been manufactured in Lancashire. Cloth of every sort and clothing, particularly luxury clothing and goods. Shoes, hats, twine, rope, buttons, rugs, pottery, quills, brass containers and much, much more went out from Lancaster. Incoming ships docked at Sunderland Point which served ships too large to sail up the river into the town. Goods were carried on lighters up the Lune and into the city centre. They brought raw cotton, sugar, tobacco, cocoa, rum and timber, and until 1833, when slavery was abolished, they brought slaves. In 1779 there were difficulties navigating up the Lune into the Port of Lancaster as the river silted up. Over many years land and buildings were purchased, and work began on the construction of a canal and the development of the small village of Glasson to build a dock. After Glasson Dock was opened in 1787, trade ships docked at Glasson. The construction of the canal, which had six locks took a long time. It was finally opened in 1830. The railway network was connected to the quay in 1883. In 1930 it became solely a goods railway. It was finally closed in 1964. The canal now has houseboats on it, and people walk dogs and ride bicycles for pleasure along its towpaths. Old warehouses have become smart blocks of flats. But it is not too much of a stretch of the imagination—enough of the old, industrial Lancaster remains—to have some idea of what it was like when Elizabeth Cock lived there.

I resolve to visit again soon and look at the maps and the archives. Next time I shall look with different eyes, searching for the past and picturing my ancestors there—particularly Elizabeth—as I walk in their footsteps.

Chapter 8

Growing Up 1959

I was thirteen in January 1959. One day I noticed a bloody stain on my knickers. I knew what it was, Mother had told me about it. I had to wear a sanitary towel which attached to an elasticated belt fastened around my waist. It was unbelievably uncomfortable to wear. When I complained, Mother said it was the best arrangement yet, better than old cloths which had to be soaked in buckets of saltwater and reused. Then there was the pain and the sickness which lasted the whole of the first day every month. I felt so ill that I had to lie down. I would vomit several times and then the next day I would be washed out and exhausted. If it happened when I was at school I had to go and lie down in the sick bay with two aspirins for the pain, then someone would bring me a school dinner on a tray. Grey mince, lumpy mash and soggy cabbage which smelled of drains; it usually made me sick again when I looked at it. If I was at home, my mother gave me Indian Brandy with hot water, which wasn't brandy at all but some stuff you bought from the chemist, and which tasted like sweet, watered down sherry. I couldn't believe how awful the whole thing was. Would this continue for the rest of my life? Mother asked the doctor about my pain and sickness. He said I'd grow out of it. I hoped he was right. The vomiting was to do with the hormones of puberty, it turns out, and nowadays would be treated. But then I just had to wait to grow out of it, which I did after a couple of years.

As a child I'd suffered from another vomiting illness for many years. It had started when I was about four. It was called cyclical vomiting and it usually lasted for several hours. I would be sick repeatedly, and even when there was nothing left to come up, I would be retching bitter bile. This would last for a day and Mother would try to make me drink water. This was after the doctor had been called one time and said that was what I needed. Then another doctor suggested a new drink called Lucozade, which I grew to hate the taste of as it reminded me of being sick. I would be left tired and weak. After a few of these attacks, Mother said she had noticed that it often happened the day before the start of a new school term. She was right but I didn't know why. I didn't mind going to school. I could do the work easily and although I only had one or two friends, I liked them very much. Looking back on this now, I suspect it was separation anxiety about leaving my home and my mother. At the time I didn't see the connection. I knew my parents loved me, I never doubted that, but Mother was undemonstrative, and Father became less so as I grew older. I was a needy and sickly child. I was often ill and had to be careful about not eating fat, which could induce violent vomiting. I was excused free school milk on these grounds. I was less sickly after I had my tonsils out when I was six. But I was in hospital for several weeks as I was a 'bleeder', a complication of tonsillectomy. I lost a lot of blood and had to have medicine and food high in iron content when I came home. I had rages and tantrums, when I screamed and cried, usually when in conflict with Father. Father slapped my legs, which made me scream even more. He would lock me in the porch until I calmed down. I had a sense of being too much for my parents, that they didn't know how to deal with me. This engendered in me an outspoken defiance that was challenging and provocative to those on the receiving end of it. The flipside of this was that I was compliant and easy-going until something triggered a rage. The middle ground of negotiation and compromise didn't feature much in my repertoire. It took a long time before I could even think about that, let alone put it into action. I know now that children's rages and tantrums need much more careful handling and should be contained and understood by a grown-up in a kind but firm manner. I didn't receive that and consequently I wasn't good at that with my own children.

Mother told me not to wash my hair when I was 'unwell', which was a nuisance. There was no reason not to wash your hair whenever you wanted but that old wives' tale prevailed until the early 1960s. You had to remember to take spare pads to school so you wouldn't get caught unawares. That happened to a girl in my class. It was in the summer and her red-and-white checked school uniform dress was soaked through with blood. And it smelled strong, the musky, metallic stink of her blood pervaded the whole classroom. Everyone noticed this and was looking around during the maths lesson to locate the source. When it ended and the teacher had left oblivious, the poor girl sat with her head on her arms on her desk, sobbing and hiding her face. After a few minutes she got up and ran out of the classroom and slunk off home. I was glad nothing like that happened to me. Even though it was an all girls school, these things weren't spoken of. We were ashamed of our bodily functions and not encouraged to talk openly. You couldn't ask anyone for help under these circumstances.

Mother went to Marks & Spencer and bought two tiny bras for me, 32A, the smallest they had for my breast buds. I put the two-bar electric fire on in my room and knelt in front of it because it was too cold to be anywhere more than a foot away from it. I held up the dainty garment with its broderie anglaise trim and examined it. It was made of white cotton. I unhooked the fasteners and held it in front of the electric fire to warm the inside of the cups. I threaded my arms through the straps and settled the cups into place over my breasts. I reached behind to fasten it and it tightened over my breasts. I stood up and looked at myself in the mirror. I was no longer a little girl; not yet a woman either, but on the way.

Along with the Mum Rollette (the first brand of commercial deodorant launched in 1958) I needed, Mother bought two booklets from Boots the chemist's: *The Reproductive Process* and *Menstruation, the Facts*. I was aware of most of what they had to say but I knew Mother was trying to be helpful and modern. She said her mother hadn't told her anything, and no one wore bras when she was young. Sometimes one of my friends came into town after school with me since I'd been catching the bus home, and we surreptitiously took other booklets off the shelf in Boots. Along with the *Home Doctor* that was on the bookshelf at home and the information that we'd learnt along the way at school and from friends, we thought we were pretty much clued-up about sex. Since I started having periods, Mother talked to me more about grown-up things.

'You know,' Mother said after one of my overnight stays at Janet's. 'Her poor mother gets depressed every six months.'

'Oh,' I said, not understanding.

'It's so bad that she can't get out of bed in the morning.'

'Janet never said anything.'

'The only thing that gets her out of it is electric shock treatment.'

'What's that?'

'It's when they give your brain a shock with electrodes on your head.'

'Strewth,' I said. This was a new expression I'd just learnt off Cathy.

'Don't use that expression, it's common,' said Mother. 'And that makes the person have a fit, like an epileptic fit.'

'Janet's cat has epileptic fits; it has tablets to control them.'

'She had those two children very close together you know,' said Mother. 'That's when it started.'

For me, these bodily changes confirmed that one day I would be able to have babies of my own. A family, that was what I'd always wanted. I had known since early childhood, when I loved bathing and playing with my dolls, that this was important to me. When Joy's mother had a baby, I pestered my own mother to have one for our family. I always wanted us to have a bigger family; more people to love and to love me, was the way I looked at it. Mother must have picked this up from me. I had a feeling—and this was to happen more often—that there was a hidden message in that conversation with Mother. She was warning me not to have babies too close together, or too soon.

At the weekends, I was often at Janet's house or she came to mine. I told her when I started my periods, and she confided in me. We updated each other on any new pieces of information about periods, sex, pregnancy, childbirth and boys. She'd caught her parents 'fucking for fun' she said one morning when she'd gone into their room. I loved the way Janet used these forbidden words. I wasn't altogether convinced that my parents did it at all never mind for fun. In fact, the idea that it was for fun was not one I had thought of before. Although I had found some condoms— 'johnnies' we called them—in my father's chest of drawers when I had a rummage around in their bedroom once when I was alone in the house. They were in the shoebox which had my father's Masonic outfit in it. They were underneath a fancy, little apron made of white kid with fabric and medals on it, and a pair of white kid gloves, all covering up the packet of johnnies. My father was important in the Masons. My parents had lots of friends who were Masons. They held a grand ball every year called a Ladies Evening when they all got dressed up. Mother would wear her marcasite jewellery and her musquash fur coat. I've learned since that this fur came from an animal called a muskrat. Would anyone have wanted to wear that fur if they knew that? The Masons was a secret society and my father said he would have his throat slit if he told me what it was about. He laughed when he said it, so I thought it was a joke, but he still didn't tell me what the secrets were. He also told me it was an insurance policy. I didn't understand what that meant but I found out later when Father needed help that the Masons, both as an organisation and as individuals, were supportive to him. Towards the end of his life he lived in a small flat that had been built by the Masons for their members, and his neighbours, ex-Masons themselves, were kind and gave regular practical help. The organisation has had some bad press since those days, but as far as my father was concerned, they were good to him when he needed help.

Janet told me about a fucking game that she played with her brother, Jeremy who was only thirteen months younger than her. She took her knickers off and lay on the bed. He took his underpants off and lay on top of her. His dick was touching her fanny.

'We can all play it when you come to stay,' she said.

'You might get pregnant,' I said.

'Don't be daft, you can't get pregnant like that.'

'It says in that booklet that even a bit of his stuff… you know… his sperm, just outside even, can swim up and get in.'

'He doesn't have any stuff, he's too little,' she said. 'It's just an experiment to see what it feels like.'

'What does it feel like?'

'Not much, it's a bit boring.'

Alongside my own developmental experiences there were events taking place which, to my eyes, seemed relatively minor, but which I now know foreshadowed something much bigger, something that would involve Father losing a great deal of money, and which were a major factor in him slowly becoming ill with depression. It was not long after my thirteenth birthday in January 1959 that I overheard my parents having frequent conversations about the cracks which had appeared on the walls and ceilings of our house. They were worst in the lounge, but all the rooms had them. Father said it was nothing to worry about, it was just the plaster drying out and the house settling.

'Sally, you know it takes a year or so for the plaster to dry out,' I heard him say one evening when Mother brought up the subject again. 'We've got to wait.'

'They look such a mess,' said Mother. 'I'm sure they shouldn't be so big. That one in the lounge seems to get wider every day.'

I was doing my homework at the dining-room table and they were standing looking at the cracks at the top of the wall between the dining room and the lounge.

'Don't exaggerate,' said Father, laughing.

'They're getting bigger, I think we should get Mr Hardcastle over, see what he has to say about it.'

'Let's see how it goes,' said Father.

I hadn't paid any attention to the cracks before, but when I looked more carefully, I saw that they did look wider. Father said a few cracks would be normal as the plaster dried out. The cracks had started off as hairline, barely discernible, but they were at least an inch or so wide in the lounge. The two alcoves and the bay window were where they were widest; it looked as if our house was pulling away from the house next door.

The relatives from Bolton came over one Sunday for tea in late February. My father's two sisters, Aunty Lizzy and Aunty Elsie were driven by Uncle George, Aunty Elsie's husband. Uncle George was a painter and decorator who didn't speak much. Aunty Elsie was thin with mousey hair which was permed and set into a hairstyle like the Queen's. Aunty Lizzy had the same hairstyle, but she wasn't so thin. They were given a tour of the cracks so George could give his opinion. He said he'd never seen anything like it, that it wasn't normal settlement, there must be something wrong. He said a decorator couldn't fill in cracks like that, it was a builder's job. For him that was a lot of talking, so it impressed everyone. Father said he'd been next door and they had similar cracks. It was the main topic of conversation while we ate our tinned salmon and salad. Jinx was hanging about around our feet. She suddenly jumped onto my knee and shot onto the table. Her nose was near Aunty Elsie's plate. Jinx moved so quickly that no one could intervene.

'Get it down,' said Aunty Elsie. 'It shouldn't be on the table.'

Uncle George leaned over, grabbed Jinx with his big hand and chucked her on the floor. Jinx stood still where she landed, her fur ruffled and her eyes big.

'Take Jinxy into the kitchen, Beth,' said Mother.

'She's upset,' I said picking her up and stroking her. I took her into the kitchen and shut the door. I could still hear them talking through the hatch. I put Jinx down and moved closer.

'Beth's certainly developed since I last saw her.' Aunty Elsie's voice drifted through. 'She's got that determined chin, you know, like Grandma's, don't you think so, Harold?'

'She was a tartar, Grandma,' said Aunty Lizzy.

'Yes, we know what she was,' said Aunty Elsie. Her voice was like sour gooseberries. 'I think Beth's going to be one of those girls with a big bust, Sally.'

I was mortified to hear them speaking of me like that. I couldn't face going back in even though Mother had made a trifle and some mandarin oranges in jelly. I took Jinx upstairs and we lay together on my bed under the eiderdown with *The Diary Of Anne Frank*. But I wasn't reading. I was thinking. Suppose I did grow up to have a big bust. I used to think I wanted a big bust like Sabrina on the Arthur Askey show. Then I thought I wouldn't if everyone was going to be gawping at me and laughing. But I didn't want an almost non-existent bust like Aunty Elsie who was thin and shapeless. I just wanted an average, normal-sized bust to suit the rest of my body. Whatever it was, I would just have to make the best of it. And my great-grandmother, who I was supposed to be like, was a tartar. What was a tartar?

I heard the hum of the relatives' voices murmuring in the hall. Mother shouted up, 'Beth, come down and say goodbye.' I pretended to be asleep and didn't answer. When they had gone, I went downstairs. Father was telling

Mother that he would get Mr Hardcastle, the builder, to come and look at the cracks.

Mr Hardcastle took his time, but when he eventually came to look he said that in his opinion it was just the plaster drying out, and normally a decorator would fill them in, but as we were worried about them, he would send a plasterer round to do the work.

'I still think we should wait before we decorate,' Father said. 'If it's like this after only six months it might settle and dry out even more in another six months.'

'I want it decorated as soon as Mr Hardcastle's plasterer has filled in all the cracks,' Mother said. 'If there's something wrong, it'll crack again and he'll have to put it right, if not... well the house will look nice.'

'That's what I mean...' said Father.

'Let's get it done, Harold. It looks such a mess.'

Father picked up some wallpaper books from Uncle George and brought them home for us to look at. I chose one with ballerinas on it for my bedroom. Father said that the plasterers would come before Easter and we would go away for a week to Devon while the house was decorated. John hadn't been home for ages, and he told Mother to choose some wallpaper for his room. Why did John stay away? I thought it was due to the animosity between him and Father, but I think he found Mother's illness difficult. I loved my big brother although he teased me unmercifully at times. The rift between him and Father would never be healed. I think Father's treatment of him as a child had been so cruel that John could never forgive him. They were also very different types of men. My father bookish and reserved, John sporty and outgoing—they had little in common. John couldn't bear to be near him. It seemed to me that John's distaste for Father overcame his love for Mother although he did come back to live at home for a while before I was married. I wished he would come home more often.

At Easter we drove down to Devon. I was excited about the holiday. Our car, a Morris Minor, was loaded up with bags, coats and jackets for all weathers. We always played games on long journeys and Father would tell stories about his relatives. When we'd exhausted I Spy and the different-makes-of-cars game, I asked him to tell me about his family. I wanted to find out more about my great-grandmother, the tartar with the determined chin.

'What about your granny?' I said. 'Where did she live?'

'There was the one that lived in Yarrow Place, my father's mother,' he said. 'Do you mean her?'

'I think so,' I said.

'She was a one, she was,' said Mother. 'Your father was her favourite when he rigged up an electric light in their outside lavatory at Yarrow Place.'

Father glanced at Mother. 'She came from Lancaster,' he said. 'She married and came to Bolton...' He had to pull in sharply as an overtaking car came towards us in the opposite direction on our side of the road. 'What's your hurry?' he said to the driver as the car whizzed past us.

'Did I go to Yarrow Place?' A dim memory was flickering in my mind like an old cine film.

'No, it was before you were born,' said Mother.

'But I remember going to see Aunt Lizzy and Grandad in another house—not where they're living now,' I said.

'That would be Horace Street,' said Father. 'Grandad went to live in Horace Street when he married your grandmother, my mother.'

'I wish I'd met her,' I said. 'My granny.'

'She was lovely, but she wasn't well when I knew her, she had a goitre,' said Mother touching her neck. 'We have a photograph taken at the back of Yarrow Place with them all on it. You can see her poor neck swollen with the goitre. I'll show it to you when we're back home.'

As I look back on this conversation, I find it remarkable that I had a sense of storing this information away for future use. I didn't know why at that time, I never questioned it, but I knew beyond any doubt that it would be helpful and important in the future. My view now is that my unconscious mind often guides me in this way.

We arrived in the evening at the village in Devon where we hoped to stay for a few nights. Father went into the pub to ask about accommodation and food. He came out and signalled for us to go in. We ate pasties and peas, then tinned peaches with clotted cream. There were no vacancies at the pub, so they recommended a place down the road. It was a new bungalow. Mother was delighted, she loved bungalows—it was her ambition to live in one.

The week in Devon passed quickly. The weather was good for the time of the year and we were able to relax on the beach, although my father still wore a suit. We enjoyed travelling around and staying in different villages and eating plenty of cream teas. I think of it now as a time of innocence, my last holiday when I was still a little girl.

There were a few days of the Easter holidays left when we came back from Devon. Cathy had gone to Wales with her family and Janet was away too. Roz rang to see if I wanted to meet her at the tennis club for a game. Mother had organised my membership and I had a new set of whites. I walked to the club in the sunshine with my racket over my shoulder. It was quiet; there were only a couple of old men playing. We had a great game. Roz was a good player, tall and strong, and she could always beat me although I wasn't bad.

'Will you come to Bury market tomorrow with me?' Roz said as we sat in the sun on the clubhouse veranda. 'I want to buy some material for my mother to make a dirndl skirt for me.'

'Yeah, that'd be great,' I said.

'We could go to Chez after for a coffee and have a look in Dorothy Perkins too.'

'What's Chez?' I said.

'Oh, haven't you been to Chez?' said Roz. 'It's a coffee bar, Chez Odette, next to the Odeon, it's great, really cool. They have live jazz upstairs on Sunday afternoons, you really must come.'

'I will.'

Roz rang up on Wednesday morning to say her mother would drive us to Bury. Mrs Ashworth dropped us off near the market and Roz took me to her favourite fabric stall.

'They always have loads of fabrics here,' she said, 'and not too expensive.'

We rummaged through the stall. There were rolls and rolls of fabric one on top of another. The stallholder pulled them out and unfurled them so we could see what the patterns were like. Roz chose some cotton fabric with a large abstract print in black and red. It looked very modern.

'Does your mother sew?' she asked.

'Yes, she makes most of my clothes,' I said.

'Mine too. Why don't you get some material?'

'I haven't got any money, well... not enough.'

'Okay, let's go and look in Dorothy Perkins. I want to get a bikini for this summer.'

I was shocked. It seems so ridiculous now to write that I was shocked by this, but bikinis were new here in staid 1950s England. Only film stars like Marilyn Monroe and Brigitte Bardot wore bikinis. I was such a prim little miss. Maybe it was my father's Methodist background. My father's family had been regular churchgoers. They attended Halliwell Road Methodist Church. My parents continued to go for some time after they married and then they stopped. After the War, church attendance generally began to drop off, but my parents continued to attend for a few years. It was certainly long enough for me to have a couple of memories of Halliwell Road Church. One is of being in some sort of show as a mouse, wearing pink-and-grey felt ears on a headband and with a long grey felt tail my mother had made. My other memory is of sitting in the church hall singing 'Jesus Wants Me for a Sunbeam'. Then we stopped going. I must have been three or four. Aunty Elsie and her family also moved away from the church; only Aunty Lizzy continued to go regularly. But the influence lingered on.

How I wanted to break away from the strait-laced little girl that I was. How boring all that was. I wanted to live, be sophisticated, be daring, try everything, wear a bikini. I couldn't wait to grow up and be free to do what I wanted to do.

Dorothy Perkins was on the way to Chez Odette. It had a stand in the middle of the shop with swimming costumes and bikinis hanging on it. Roz and I browsed through them. Roz picked out a blue-and-white striped one that would suit her colouring. I picked out a cerise gingham one with white broderie anglaise trimming.

'What do you think?' I held the bikini bottoms next to my face.

'It suits you,' said Roz.

I looked in a full-length mirror that was near the curtained-off cubicle where you could try clothes on. I was small like my mother, five feet two inches, although she was size twelve now and I was size eight, or sometimes a six. My hair was chestnut brown and my eyes dark brown. My skin was north country, English pale and I had the remains of one or two spots on my chin. Someone at school told me I was the prettiest girl in the class, but I wasn't sure about that.

'Do you want to try that on, love?' said the assistant. 'Only if you do, try it on over your knickers.'

'Oh no, thank you,' I said.

'Try it on,' said Roz. 'Go on.'

I went into the cubicle and tried it on. The little bra top was cut to push my breasts up and the bottoms stretched over my backside in a perfect fit. My hip bones jutted out at each side of my stomach. Roz called through the curtain. 'Have you got it on?'

'Yes.'

'Let's see.' She poked her head round the curtain. '*C'est parfait, mademoiselle, comme Brigitte Bardot.*'

'*Tu penses?*' I said.

'*Oui, oui, oui, ooh là,*' said Roz. We giggled and she

withdrew her head.

I thought of the bathing costume I wore in Devon. It was a dull blue, a little girl's costume with gathers across the front. I could never wear that again. I must have this bikini. I dressed and came out of the cubicle.

'Well?' said Roz.

'You're right, it's perfect.'

'You'll have to have it,' said Roz.

'I know, I'll have to ask my mother though…'

Chez Odette was part of the Odeon Cinema building on the corner of the street. It had the same Art Deco style as the cinema and its metal-framed windows followed the curve of the building. Inside, it was all pale green, black and chrome with cream imitation leather bench seats under the window. But it wasn't smart, the fabric was scuffed and had a few tears. There was a hint of faded glamour to it, like a 1930s film star grown old. Its tawdriness was part of its appeal to the teenagers, drop-outs, musicians and odd-looking people who frequented it. You could imagine you were in Paris in some Left Bank dive hanging out with a bohemian crowd. The space was small, wedge-shaped, like a slice of the apple pie that was displayed in a glass cabinet under the high bar in the corner. Odette was a Belgian woman with dark skin, jet black hair and a strong accent, who had somehow fetched up in Bury. Odette and her husband dispensed coffee from the first espresso coffee machine I'd ever seen. They had regular slanging matches in loud and rapid French. As far as we could tell he accused her of flirting with the customers. Their arguments were one of the many attractions of the place. There were numerous small Formica tables and metal chairs that you had to squeeze past to get to the bar. Roz and I sat in the window seat where you had a good view of the rest of the customers as well as being able to see who was walking past. You ordered at the bar and then sat down. Roz ordered espresso coffee and a slice of apple pie, and I ordered the same. My spending money was rapidly diminishing. I'd got enough for the bus fare home and that was it.

'They're having a party next door in a couple of weeks,' said Roz as we tucked into our apple pie. 'You know, the Browns.'

'Oh, what for? Something special?'

'It's Linda's birthday, she's sixteen. That's why I've got the material for a new skirt. I've got a new blouse to wear with it. You could come if you want, they won't mind.'

'But I don't know her,' I said.

'That won't matter, they're used to having lots of people around. They've got five kids and they all take their friends... in fact, why don't you come over tomorrow and we'll go around to their house. Perhaps we could go to the pictures as well.'

'Is there anything good on?'

'Let's look on our way back. And we could call in the record shop and listen to some records, you know, pretend we're going to buy some then walk out, or we could go into Woolworth's and look at the make-up.' Roz looked at my unmade-up face. 'I'll make you up if you want as well.' She opened her bag and pulled out two cigarettes. 'Do you want a fag?'

Chapter 9
Yarrow Place 1901

I have an old photograph of my father as a boy. There are other members of his family on it. It has been in a box among family holiday snaps, formal school portraits and other photographs of our lives for as long as I can remember. On the back in faded ink and neat, flowing handwriting, are the words *Yarrow Place 1926*. This is the photograph my mother referred to while we were driving to Devon in 1959. She kept her word and showed it to me when we returned home. I've had it safe ever since, knowing I would need it some day. There are eight people in this tiny photograph. I vaguely remember who is who from Mother telling me. I recognise the boy standing at the back, with his hand on the shoulder of an old lady—it is my father. He was born in 1910 and would have been about sixteen when this photograph was taken.

The old lady is my great-grandmother, Elizabeth Cock, the tartar. I do a quick calculation in my head. She would have been seventy-two. She looks more like ninety-two. She is tiny, shrunken. Her white hair is tied up in a wispy knot of a bun on top of her head. The man on the back row of the photograph is Grandad Cox, Albert Edward. I recognise him from his moustache. Between my father and grandfather are two young women. They are Aunt Elsie and Aunt Lizzy. Elsie was two years older than Father and Lizzy two years younger. They look about the right age. There are three women sitting in front of them, other than my great-grandmother. One is obviously the grandmother I never met, my father's mother, the one with the goitre. She is wearing a scarf around her neck, but it has slipped, and the goitre is plainly visible. Of the two women next to her, one I think is Great-aunt Annie. She has a kitten on her knee. Father said they always had a cat called Tiddles. So, who is this other woman? And where is Cyril? Cyril, my father's younger brother was killed when he was twenty-one in Italy during the Second World War, but he was born in 1921, so he would have been about five when this photograph was taken. And who took the photograph? It's not a studio portrait; it's just an amateur snapshot. Not for the first time, I wish I had questioned my parents and my aunts.

A few years after Grandad died, Aunt Lizzy moved to a new bungalow. The photograph in the gold frame of Great-grandmother Elizabeth Cock was now hanging on the wall of Aunt Lizzy's bungalow in the lounge. I thought I'd ask again about Elizabeth.

'That's Grandma,' said Aunty Lizzy. Her voice had a tone of disapproval in it.

'What was she like?' I said.

'She was a tyrant. She had her daughters doing the housework.' Aunty Lizzy's tone of disapproval darkened; it was *vehement* with disgust. Great-grandmother was a tyrant as well as a tartar. A tyrannical tartar. I felt somehow that I was being disapproved of. It stopped me from asking any more. Why was she so disgusted? And who are the daughters Aunty Lizzy referred to? As far as I know Great-grandmother Elizabeth only had one, Great-aunt Annie.

I go to my laptop to search for more answers. The 1901 census has no sign of Elizabeth Cock nor of any other family members in Britannia Street. Where is Elizabeth now? Has she married? I start a search through the Births, Marriages and Deaths. Here it is. In 1892, Elizabeth Margaret Cock married John Goulburn of Bolton in St Thomas' Church in the centre of Lancaster, where Elizabeth, and her brothers and sisters, were christened. I search for her under her new name, Elizabeth Goulburn. In 1901 she is living in 31 Yarrow Place, Bolton. It's all alive in front of me, falling into place. Yarrow Place—I love the old-fashioned sound of it—and... I can hardly believe it... Elizabeth is a widow. And she has Albert Edward and Annie living there with her, their surnames are now Cox, and... there are four others there too. Four grown-up Goulburn children. Ellen, Bessie, Frank and William. *She had her daughters doing the housework.*

These are the daughters. They were John Goulburn's children from his first marriage. Elizabeth and John both brought their children to the marriage. It must have seemed like a godsend to Elizabeth. A move to a new town where she could be a respectable married woman. He was a widower; maybe if anyone asked, she could play the part of remarried widow. In any case it would all look respectable. Her two illegitimate children could change their names from the hated Cock to Cox. Great-aunt Annie could call herself Goulburn and pretend she was part of John's family. That was what she told me her maiden name was all those years ago, Annie Goulburn. Was John Goulburn Annie's father? Or was Annie attempting to legitimise herself by using Goulburn? Mother and Father both told me that Annie carried a great burden of shame about her illegitimacy throughout her life, and that was the reason she didn't get married until she was forty. I never fully understood what they meant by that—another story I wished I had asked more about.

I search for John Goulburn in the Births, Marriages and Deaths. His first marriage was to Mary Ann in 1876. At the time of the 1881 census, John and Mary Ann Goulburn are living at 21 Upper Pen Street, Little Bolton, with their three oldest children. Mary Ann died in 1888 at the age of 41, so John and Mary Ann's fourth child must have been born between 1881 and 1888. Here's a clue. Mary Ann was born in Lancaster. Is that the connection with Elizabeth? Mary Ann's family in Lancaster? By the time of the 1901 census, John is dead. In fact, I discover that he died in 1897, so he was only married to Elizabeth for five years. She remained in Yarrow Place until her death in 1930. Birth, death and marriage certificates can be ordered at the Registry Office in the relevant town, although you can do it through

Ancestry.co.uk as well.

Great-grandmother Elizabeth had living with her the four Goulburn children, who were of working age. The oldest three worked as cotton weavers, as did Annie Goulburn/Cox. William, the youngest Goulburn, was a saddler's apprentice. My grandfather, Albert Edward Cox, was a bricklayer. Elizabeth was the housekeeper. She must have been reasonably well-off at this point. Even though she had lost her husband, materially life had improved. The marriage to John Goulburn had been a new start, a chance to leave the shameful history of illegitimacy behind in Lancaster. Now she had inherited John Goulburn's house and family.

The photograph that I have of all those people taken at Yarrow Place looks to be taken at the back of a Victorian house. I know they had a backyard with their own outside toilet, where my father had installed an electric light. It may have been a terraced house or a semi-detached house, but it looks substantial. It's not the slum that Britannia Street was with its row of stinking privies in a communal courtyard and its dank alleyways.

I look through my A–Z of Greater Manchester, not expecting to find Yarrow Place, but I do. It's still there. I must see it. I stop and think for a moment—nothing else needs my attention, it's two o'clock in the afternoon, the traffic won't be too busy. Why not go now?

I navigate my way there, darting glances at the A–Z on the passenger seat. As I approach the area where Yarrow Place is situated, I smile. There is the dome of a mosque rising above the skyline of house roofs. I think of Aunt Lizzy, the Methodist churchgoer, who was profoundly racist. My father had owned a little terraced house in this neighbourhood many years ago and when his long-term tenant moved out, he sold it to a Pakistani man. Aunt Lizzy was shocked, disturbed and furious about this. I know this because she told me; I suppose she felt she could say these things because she assumed I felt the same. I didn't, and I tried to reason with her about it but she wouldn't listen; it was utter, blind prejudice.

The Victorian houses on Yarrow Place have gone. In their place are newish terraces. The streets around are busy, lively, with shops whose pavement stalls spill over with colourful vegetables and fruit. The people in the streets are mainly of Asian origin, walking, shopping, pushing prams, living their lives. The women wear shalwar kameez and saris of bright turquoise and fuchsia pink. The men wear white cotton trousers and long cotton overshirts. Some old men have hennaed beards and wear little white hats. I smile again as I think about how Aunt Lizzy would have reacted to the street scene. I am disappointed that the old house is no longer here, and I can't somehow fit that dark Victorian house into the Yarrow Place of today. It's gone but I'm making sure it isn't forgotten.

There's something nagging at the back of my mind. It is to do with Elizabeth and her life, and the way things turned out for her. I have a feeling that misfortune befell her birth family, just as it did mine. I have an uncanny sense of being tuned into her, connected in some way that I don't yet know. But I will find out. I want to understand her and this, I know, is the way to understanding myself.

Chapter 10

Smoking, Shopping and Make-up 1959

I went over to Roz's the next day and, as I walked past the Browns' house, I noticed a girl sitting on the low wall surrounding their garden. She looked about sixteen and had a huge bouffant, blonde hairstyle. She was wearing a full-skirted, cotton dress and a pair of the highest and thinnest heeled stiletto shoes, they must have been at least four inches high. She had a white miniature poodle on a lead. She was saying, 'Sit,' and pushing its bottom down. Every time she stopped pushing it down it stood up again. When it saw me, it started barking and dancing around on the end of its lead. The girl looked up.

'This dog's bloody stupid, I can't get it to sit,' she said to me. Her blue eyes looked as if they were laughing. 'I'm giving up on this, I think I'll just take it for a walk instead.'

I heard a door banging. Roz appeared from behind the shrubs that separated the two gardens.

'Hi, Roz,' said the girl.

'Hi Linda,' said Roz. 'Did I hear you say you're going for a walk?'

'Yeah, I'm taking the dog.'

'Beth and I are going for the bus; we'll walk with you.' Roz smiled at me. 'Okay?' I nodded.

'So, you're Beth,' said the girl. She looked me up and down.

'Hello,' I said feeling a rush of blood to my face. Her gaze made me feel embarrassed, as if I wasn't up to scratch.

'Well, let's go then,' said Roz.

'I've got a problem,' Linda addressed Roz as we walked. She seemed to have no difficulty in walking on her high heels. 'I've got two boys after me and I don't know which one I want.'

'What a terrible problem.' Roz nudged me with her

elbow. 'So, which one are you going to invite to your party?'

'I'll invite them both and see what happens,' said Linda laughing. She had a deep and throaty laugh, a dirty laugh. 'Do you feel like helping me with the food on the day?'

'Yeah, I don't mind, what are you doing?'

'I don't know, just salad and stuff, I suppose, ham, salad and bread rolls, stuff like that. The parents are going away for the weekend to the caravan and taking the little kids with them, so we'll have the house to ourselves.'

'Beth can come, can't she? She'll help with the food.' Roz gave me another nudge, but I couldn't find my voice. I nodded.

'Yeah.' I received another glance from the laughing blue eyes. 'I've got a new dress, it's black and fitted, so sexy.' Linda gave a shimmy with her body and laughed.

'Mother's making me a skirt,' said Roz. We had reached the bus stop. They both looked at me.

'What about you?' said Linda.

'Will this do?' I felt flustered. I looked down at my dress which Mother had made. It had puff sleeves and a Peter Pan collar. The fabric was pale pink with small white dogs on it. A little girl's dress. I looked at them both. Linda wore coral lipstick. It really suited her. Her blue eyeshadow was barely there but it perfectly complemented her eyes. Her blonde hair colour was natural-looking, she looked sophisticated. Roz's make-up was less perfectly applied, her mascara had clumped up a bit, but her height and her natural Scandinavian-type beauty made her look older.

'Have you got anything else?' said Linda.

'I'll… I'll have a look,' I said.

'We'll have a hair and make-up session before the party,' said Roz. 'Cathy will be back from Wales tomorrow, so we'll do it then.'

The next afternoon at Roz's house, Roz and Cathy put an auburn rinse from Woolworth's on my hair and set it in rollers. Then we chose from the various eyeshadows and Max Factor pancake make-up they had between them. I'd brought along my own new black mascara. We played records on Roz's record player and we sang along using a hairbrush as a microphone. Cathy broke into a sort of operatic rendition of *Blueberry Hill* to make us laugh. I was sitting in front of Roz's chest of drawers, which had a mirror above it. Cathy was brushing out my hair. I had Cathy's green eyeshadow on and her foundation. My skin was lighter than either of theirs, and I didn't like the green eyeshadow much, but I was enjoying myself. Roz came in with three mugs of coffee.

'Your hair looks great,' said Roz. My hair had come out of the rollers in glossy waves. 'Here.' She threw me a cigarette. I'd refused the one she'd offered me in Chez. It was too public for my first one. I picked this one up and held it between my fingers. It had a tip.

'I've never had one before,' I said. 'What's this for?' I touched the tip.

'It stops you getting tobacco in your mouth,' said Roz.

'It looks cool,' said Cathy.

I put it to my mouth and in an exaggerated gesture pretended to inhale and blow out smoke. We giggled. Roz struck a match, lit Cathy's cigarette and then came to me. I just held the cigarette in the flame. We giggled again.

'You can't light it like that. Put it in your mouth, hurry up, it's burning my fingers.' Roz blew the match out as we all folded up giggling. She threw the match in a large ashtray which was on the floor and already nearly full of cigarette ends.

'Okay, let's try again,' said Roz. 'This time put it in your mouth and suck.'

This time I sucked in a little and the cigarette lit. I coughed and blew out the smoke pulling a face.

'Ugh, I don't like it,' I said, shivering.

'You won't at first,' said Cathy. 'It takes time, you've got to persevere.'

I struck a pose, legs crossed, cigarette between my fingers and looked down my nose at them. I had another puff on the cigarette, it went to the back of my throat this time and I coughed and coughed. I shivered again.

'Ugh, I think I might be sick,' I said. Cathy and Roz fell back laughing on Roz's bed. I took in some deep breaths of the stale bedroom air and managed to recover. I put the cigarette, hands-free, so that it dangled out of the corner of my mouth and looked at them mock serious. I nearly choked as I started laughing and the smoke and the laughing made me cough again. Roz hung her cigarette in the corner of her mouth and let it dangle there. She was clearly an expert.

'Here's lookin' at ya, kid,' she put on an American accent. Cathy tried to do the same, but her cigarette fell out of her mouth onto the carpet.

'Oh no.' She picked up the cigarette and rubbed at the carpet where it had landed.

'You can't do much harm to this carpet,' said Roz. 'It's ancient and I don't know when it was last hoovered.'

'The next lesson is how to inhale,' said Cathy.

'Can I save that for next time? I do feel a bit sick,' I said.

Cathy took a coffee cup to the bathroom and brought me some water. I took a sip. I still felt queasy. Smoking wasn't as easy as it looked. There was a lot more to learn. Inhaling, blowing out smoke rings, blowing smoke down your nose and letting a cigarette dangle out of your mouth hands-free for more than just a second. Generally, you were wanting to look cool and casual without choking to death. It all needed a lot of practice. Roz and Cathy could steal or beg fags from their parents, but Mother had never smoked, and Father had given up his Passing Clouds, the elegant, oval-shaped cigarettes that he always used to have on his desk in our old house, in their pink box of fifty. I needed to buy fags as my contribution towards these smoking sessions occasionally. A packet of five Senior Service cost just over a shilling. It was one of the strongest brands apart from Capstan Full Strength, but you could only buy those in tens and twenties. The stronger, the cooler.

What with smoking practice, make-up, updating my wardrobe, travelling on buses, and drinking coffee and eating apple pie in Chez, my three shillings-a-week pocket money wasn't nearly enough to cover all my expenses. I thought about how to raise money. I had four guinea pigs that lived in a cage in the garage. I advertised them and their cage on a noticeboard we had at school. That raised four pounds and I broke into my League of Pity collecting box, which was full of pennies. It only amounted to three shillings and seven pence. Obviously, this extra money wouldn't last long. I needed to ask for an increase in pocket money. I had a feeling it wouldn't go down too well, but I couldn't keep putting it off. I found an opportunity when Mother was washing up on Friday evening. I picked up a tea towel and started drying the pots.

'Oh, thank you, Beth,' she said, giving me a smile.

'I'm going into town tomorrow with Roz,' I said.

'Again?' said Mother.

'Yes, so, can I have my spending money please?'

'I'll give it to you after.'

'I could do with a rise, a bit more.'

'What for?'

'There's the bus fare and we'll probably go for a coffee to Chez and... I thought I'd look at material on the market... and I'd like to try on the blouses and bikinis in Dorothy Perkins as well.'

My mother stopped washing up and looked at me with a shocked expression on her face. 'A blouse, material and a *bikini*?'

'What's wrong with that?' I said.

'A *bikini*,' she repeated. 'I've just bought you a new tennis skirt and top... anyway you've got a swimming costume.'

'I can't wear that any more, it's too small.'

'You're far too young for a bikini, Beth,' said Mother. 'In any case, it's only common girls who wear them. No, you mustn't even think of it.'

'Everyone else has got one, it's not fair.' I threw down the tea towel and ran upstairs to my bedroom where I flung myself on the bed and cried a few tears of frustration. Soon I heard Mother coming up. She knocked on the door and put her head round.

'Beth,' she said. She came and sat on the bed. She looked down at the pale green cotton bedspread, which she had made. She stroked it.

'The thing is one way and another, money's a bit tight now. We've just put some more into the business. I didn't want to... but, well your father thought we should... so anyway... I was going to start sewing again, you know earn some money by making curtains and loose covers for people. I can do it from home with my sewing machine, but...' She stopped and looked so upset that I felt guilty. She was quiet for a minute. 'I saw the consultant last week and I'm... probably going to need more treatment, I've got backache and... so, we'll have to see...' She smiled at me, she was being brave, I knew. I didn't understand what she meant but I could see that she was upset underneath her smile, so I thought I shouldn't ask.

I stayed in my room lying on my bed. I didn't want my mother to be ill again. I knew she'd been resting a lot, but I thought it was just that she hadn't recovered from her operation. I couldn't understand why she had a problem with her back. It didn't make any sense to me and I had that feeling again, that this wasn't the whole story. She didn't want to tell me so it must be serious, something new. I thought I might ask Father about it. Life seemed to be getting more complicated. Here was I, wanting to break free from my parents and their restricted lives, and they were becoming ill and having money problems.

I rang Roz to talk about the pocket money situation and she reckoned that fathers were more amenable to these sorts of requests than mothers. I decided to approach Father one evening after tea. He was sitting in the dining room reading his French translation of *David Copperfield*. His interest in French had been triggered when as a young man he went to

Paris with a friend. He loved Paris but was frustrated at not being able to speak French. He was determined thereafter to learn the language and it became a lifelong passion for him. He had a glass of whisky on the table next to him. Mother was watching television in the front room. I was trying to do my chemistry homework at the dining-room table. I had no interest in it and my mind kept wandering off. I went and sat on the rug next to Father. Jinx was lying there stretched out. I stroked her cream underbelly. It was velvet soft.

'Have you finished your homework?' said Father.

'Nearly.'

'Do you need some help?'

'No... well, it's okay,' I said. I stroked Jinx some more. 'Has Mother said anything to you?'

'What about?' he said.

'Well... you know my friends Roz and Cathy? We go shopping and we go on the bus to the cinema...'

'And it all costs money,' he said with a smile. 'I know. How much do you need?'

'I was wondering about an increase in pocket money... but, Mother said that the business is a bit...'

'Don't worry, trade will pick up soon, business is like that, up and down,' he said. 'I don't think an increase in pocket money will break the bank.'

I got up and kissed him on his cheek. 'Thanks.' He smiled at me. I sat down again on the rug.

'Is Mother all right?' I said.

'Why do you ask?' he said.

'She told me she might need more treatment.'

'Hmm, that's how it's looking at the moment.'

'I don't understand,' I said. 'She said it's her back, is it something different?'

Father sighed and put down his book. 'Well, Beth,' he paused and stroked my hair. I leaned against his legs. 'You're growing up very quickly now,' he stopped for a moment. 'I'll try to explain...' He was quiet, thinking what to say, how to tell me something difficult. 'I think the best way is to tell you... your Mother has... she has something called cancer.'

'What's that?' I had never heard the word before.

'Well, it's a growth, a group of malignant cells that occur in the body, that's what the lump was in her breast. They took as much of it away as they could, but it had already spread. You see, it can spread anywhere in the body, so that's what they think might be the problem with her back, that the cancer has spread.'

'Ugh, that sounds awful,' I said. I imagined tentacles of cancer spreading around Mother's body, weaving and worming their way into and around her bones. I shivered. 'So, what can they do?'

'Probably something called deep X-ray treatment.'

'What's that?'

'Well, it's a way of sending rays into the body to destroy the cancer. It's a very strong treatment and it can destroy good tissue as well, so it's...' his voice trailed off. He cleared his throat. 'It's not without problems, we'll just have to see how it goes for her. It may make her more ill for a little while when she has it.' He stroked my hair again. 'We'll all have to help as much as we can.'

I sat still, leaning into Father's legs, looking at the fire and stroking Jinx. I felt miserable. Why was everything going wrong? I wanted life to go back to what it was before we moved. I wanted my mother back. I looked down at the fitted Turkish carpet that Mother had chosen for the hall and dining room. It was a deep red with a blue design on it, 'pub and club' carpet, Aunt Elsie had called it when she saw it. I hated her for saying that. It was Mother's carpet, she'd chosen it. A flame flickered in me. I felt the heat of it as fury raged around my body. It was at Aunt Elsie, at my stupid chemistry homework, at Father, at Mother, at having to move to a new house, at everything. I stood up. I felt like throwing something, smashing something up. I looked around. The fire irons were close to hand, there were some ornaments on the fireplace and a clock. But I couldn't do

82

that, it would upset Father and Jinx. So, I got up and threw my schoolbooks into my satchel, tearing one of them in the process, and went upstairs to bed.

Chapter 11
Britannia Street 1871

Now that I know what happened to Elizabeth Cock, how she married John Goulburn and ended up in Bolton, I am keen to learn more about her family background. I must find some reason for my sense that something went awry in her family. I suspect there are reasons why Elizabeth followed an unconventional route especially at a time when illegitimacy was regarded as very shameful for both mother and child. There is probably more than one reason, and it could be complex. Double standards prevailed and, for some men, women could serve as convenient receptacles for unwanted parts of themselves. So, the women became bad, wanton, weak, lacking in moral fibre, while the men were none of these things. They were entitled to have what they believed they needed. There can also be many threads that come together in one person; one member of a family may represent or carry something for the others. I see now that, coming as I did after the War, I must have been the embodiment of hopes for the future, a new world where women could do as they wanted, have careers, be independent, enjoy sex, have fun. I see something in Elizabeth that I identify with. It's almost as if I am her at times, so strong is my sense of identification with her. As if something of her has been passed down the generations into me.

This family history research is such an important investigation for me. It's an obsession. It is as if my whole life has brought me to this point. It's all been waiting for me. Elizabeth has been waiting for me to tell her story to a world that may now be ready to receive it. For me too, it's time to tell my story and all this is the portal to the new place in myself and my life that I am groping towards. The boxes that have waited in the back of my head contain clues to the hidden past that people before me felt tainted by, damaged by and ashamed of, and wanted to disown. I'm bringing them out and opening them to the light of the twenty-first century. It's fallen to me to face the past and examine what happened and why. And perhaps through facing my family's past, I can face my own and not be ashamed of it.

The search for Albert and Annie's father(s) has brought no results. I must accept that I may never know who he was, or who they were. There are no clues to follow up, but no matter, my search for him was incidental to my other more pressing search, which is to find out more about Elizabeth. I know that something went seriously wrong. I think she's been maligned and misunderstood, and I think that over one hundred years later I have, at times, been judged in much the same way. I realise as I write that I have judged myself. I'm doing this for her and also for myself.

So, I'm in Lancaster again delving into the past. It's 1871. The Cock family are living in Britannia Street. Mother Esther is forty-five, a widow and housekeeper. She has her six children living with her. Elizabeth is eighteen, working as a cotton-carder, as is Catherine, aged sixteen. Christopher at twelve is a grocer's errand boy. The three younger children who are described as scholars are Esther, nine, William, seven, and Mary Ellen, five. Mary Ellen, I have not met before. This means that their father, William must have died in the last six years or so, leaving Esther alone with their six children to bring up. Elizabeth would have been aged around twelve, but possibly old enough to work otherwise Esther would have had no income. How did she manage? Her children must have had to find jobs, perhaps part-time work, but it would not have been much. They must have been poor. Growing up in these conditions would have been hard. I am surprised yet again by the depth of feeling I experience regarding my ancestors. This is heartbreaking. I also see as I write that Elizabeth and I both experienced significant changes in our lives at around the same time, when we were going through puberty and adolescence. It's another of the uncanny parallels between Elizabeth and me.

Chapter 12
The Party 1959

I went around to the Browns' house on Saturday afternoon to help prepare food for Linda's party. Mother had agreed that I could stay over at Roz's house. Roz and I listened to records as we worked in the Browns' big kitchen. An LP of Elvis singing all the songs from the film *Jailhouse Rock* was playing. We sang along as we spread butter onto white bread rolls and made open sandwiches with ham and tomatoes, and egg and cress. We broke off for a few minutes to practise our jiving steps. We sang as we twirled around, before continuing to place Lancashire cheese on a bread board with cream crackers and celery sticks in a jug of water. Linda directed operations. As each plate was finished, it was put on the dining-room table with bowls of crisps and covered with tea towels ready for the evening. Sausage rolls were to be heated in the oven later and there was a big birthday cake from a confectioner in Bury. Cathy didn't turn up to help. Roz said she probably had to do her piano practice.

'You know what their parents are like?' she said.

'What do you mean?' I said.

'They push them all to study, Cathy's good at music so she's never allowed off her piano practice, and Gareth, poor Gareth, he's hardly ever been allowed to go out, it's been all Oxford, Oxford, Oxford.'

Adrian came into the kitchen carrying a big cardboard box. 'Do you want these here?' He inclined his head towards the table.

'Yeah, I think so,' said Linda. 'Drinks are always in the kitchen at parties. What've you got there?'

'Cider, Babycham, lemonade, Vimto.' Adrian pulled the bottles out and put them on the table. 'Have we got enough glasses?'

'Probably not.' Linda opened a cupboard.

'I'm sure the parents won't mind if I bring some of ours,' said Roz.

'I'll go and look in the dining-room cupboard.' Linda went off.

Adrian turned to me. 'What do you drink, little miss?' He smiled.

'Oh, Vimto probably,' I said.

'You might try a Babycham tonight.' He winked at me.

'I might,' I said, feeling my face flush.

Roz and I left to get changed into our party clothes. By a stroke of good luck, Aunt Lizzy had given Mother a skirt to alter for me. It was one she had bought for herself but decided she didn't like. It was the most sophisticated garment I had ever owned; the fabric was black with a pattern of tan-coloured roses on it. I had won the battle of the blouse by forgoing the bikini, so I had a new white, scoop-necked blouse to wear with it. I cinched it all together with a wide black belt around my waist. Shoes had been another problem. The only shoes I possessed were little girls' sandals and school shoes which I wore with ankle socks. Neither were suitable to wear with this new grown-up outfit. I had been staring at and lusting over a pair of shoes in the Dolcis shop window for a few days as I walked to the bus station after school before the holidays. They were black with kitten heels and pointed toes. They were priced at £4 19s 6d. I had been careful with my small amount of pocket money, and with the cash from the guinea pig sale I had enough to buy them. Roz and I made a trip to Bolton on the Friday afternoon before the party so I could try them on. They squashed up my toes, but I didn't care one bit. I knew Mother would go mad when she saw them, but I didn't care about that either. They were my first pair of grown-up heels. With the addition of make-up, I felt suitably dressed and consequently more confident.

There were a few people at the party by the time Roz and I arrived. I didn't know any of them apart from Linda and Adrian, and Gareth and Cathy. They all looked older and more sophisticated than me at still only thirteen. I felt Cathy ignored me and took Roz to one side. Gareth and I were left standing together.

'Do you want a drink?' he said.

'Yes, please,' I said.

'What do you want?'

I shrugged my shoulders. I was out of my depth and tongue-tied. My new confidence was seeping away.

'Why don't you sit there, and I'll choose something for you,' he said pointing to a small sofa in a corner of the large sitting room. It was near to the record player, so I sat down and looked at the LPs the Browns had piled up there. I didn't own even one LP. My few records were singles, not even EPs. From the record player, the Everley brothers were singing 'Bird Dog'. I didn't know what it meant but I felt myself relax as I sat there listening to the music and drinking the Babycham that Gareth brought back for me. The bubbles went straight to my head. I felt giddy, happy, grown-up. I crossed my legs and looked at my new shoes. I wished my legs weren't so white. Adrian came over to change the record.

'You're looking very pretty tonight, Miss Cox,' he said grinning. 'Let's get you another of those.'

He took my glass off me. I smiled back with my new Babycham-fuelled confidence.

'Adrian flirts with all the girls,' said Gareth. 'He's okay though.'

Adrian returned with a glass for me. 'I've put something else in there to give it a kick,' he said. 'Tell me if you like it.'

I tasted it. I could tell there was something else in it, it was stronger, more flavoursome.

'Yes, I do,' I nodded and smiled.

Gareth and I talked about his A levels. He was taking physics, chemistry and maths this year, but he was waiting another year before going to Oxford. He told me that he was nearly seventeen and would be taking his driving test soon. I talked about why I had come to live in Holcombe Brook, and he told me about Roz and Cathy's close friendship, the railway line and his photography. The time slipped by and the Babychams kept arriving and slipping down my throat, I noticed Adrian move towards the door with one of the older girls. He was holding her hand. Adrian glanced around as he left the room, grinning.

'He's taking her upstairs to bed,' said Gareth. He put his arm along the back of the sofa behind me.

'Really?' I said. My voice came out thick. I stood up. 'I think... I think... I'd better find the toilet.'

'Are you all right?' said Gareth.

'No.' The room was spinning round, and I felt sick.

'Let's get you outside,' said Gareth. 'The fresh air will make you feel better.' He took me by the arm and guided me into the back garden. We stood for a moment at the back door. I swayed and staggered to the low wall which bordered the path. I leant over the wall and threw up.

'Oh,' I moaned. 'Sorry.'

'Don't worry,' said Gareth. 'I didn't think you'd had that much. I wonder what Adrian put in it?'

'I've never had Babycham before. Oh, I feel awful.' I threw up again and sat down on the wall. I wiped my mouth with my hand. I looked up at him. He smiled.

'I'll make you a coffee, it'll sober you up before you go home.'

'I'm shtaying at Roz's,' I said in a strange, thick voice. My tongue had trouble articulating the words and they came out slurred. I started to laugh, and Gareth joined in. He put his arm round me.

'Could you eat anything? That might help.'

'Water, just water.' I leaned over the wall and threw up again.

'Okay. I'll get a glass of water. Wait here.'

He came back with the water and a rug. I sipped the water, and it tasted delicious as it gurgled into my empty stomach. I moved off the wall to lie down on the lawn which felt dry and cool. I lay on my back and looked up at the stars in the dark blue night sky. The stars wouldn't stay still, they moved dizzyingly round and round then slid away to one side.

'Look,' I pointed upwards. 'I can shee the Plough, but it won't stay shtay shtill.'

Gareth laughed. I turned on my side and curled up. He placed the rug over me and lay down next to me. He snuggled his body round mine under the rug and put his arm around me. The sounds of music and the murmur of people's voices, with the occasional loud laughter drifted out to us on the lawn. I relaxed into his warmth and we lay like that, his body wrapped round mine under the blanket, until Roz came to get me when it was time to leave.

Back at school for the summer term, I was late leaving on Wednesdays, as I had to go to rounders practice. I'd been chosen for the under-fourteen team. We had swimming on Wednesdays too and so I was standing in the bus station waiting for the later bus with my swimming gear rolled up in a towel under my arm. It was quiet, not many people around. A man came and stood behind me in the queue. He was an ordinary-looking man about my father's age. When I thought about him later, I could only remember that he was unremarkable. He was of medium height and weight, his hair was a mid-brown colour, cut in a short back and sides. I could not recall any distinguishing features about him. But what he said and how he made me feel was horrible. There was no one else in the bus queue, and after a while he spoke to me.

'Been swimming?'

'Yes,' I said.

'Do you like swimming?'

'No, not really—the pool's too cold.'

'Do you ever have to miss swimming?'

I didn't know what he meant, and I felt uncomfortable, so I didn't answer.

'I expect you're too young yet, but you'll have a good excuse when you start your periods,' he said.

I looked around to see if there was a woman nearby. I thought I could tell a woman what he was saying to me. But there weren't any. In fact, the whole bus station was quiet. There was a man in the distance but otherwise there seemed to be no one around. I started to feel panicky, I didn't know what to do. I had just missed a bus, so I had nearly half an hour to wait for the next one.

'What's your bathing costume like?' he said. 'What colour is it?'

'Blue,' I said.

'Does it reveal much?'

I stood there feeling frightened and helpless.

'What's the matter? Don't you want to talk to me?'

I was near to tears and didn't know what to say. A boy joined the queue and another man. I was wondering if I should say something to this other man, but I couldn't bring myself to do it. At least the presence of these other people had the effect of shutting up the first man. But I began to worry that he would sit next to me on the bus. Suppose he got off at the same stop as me and followed me? It would be quiet down Longsight Road at this time. The shops would be closed. Maybe I could knock on someone's door but suppose no one answered? I would be cornered in someone's garden. I stood there feeling desperate. It seemed a long time until the bus came. I'd had time to think through what to do so I sat on the front seat near the driver and I put my bag on the seat beside me. The man walked past without a glance and sat further down the bus. But that didn't stop me worrying. Throughout the half-hour journey, I worried about him following me when I got off the bus. What a relief when he stayed on after my stop. As I walked down Longsight Road, I tried to work out what to do if anything like that happened again but in my panicked state of mind, I couldn't think of anything. I walked home feeling sick with anxiety.

They seemed to be everywhere, these dirty old men. We were warned that same week by the headmistress in assembly not to walk through the nearby park alone. She said it wasn't safe. The story went around school that a man had jumped out and flashed at the head girl.

A couple of weeks after that, Janet came to stay for the weekend. On the Saturday it was a mild and sunny late spring day. We decided to explore the fields at the bottom of my road. We climbed over a stile in the hedge and walked across the field to a little stream with a wooden bridge. It was partially hidden by bushes and a copse of blackthorn. The sun sparkled the white flowers on the black twigs. We lolled about on the bridge watching the water as it flowed underneath. Janet, who was good at gymnastics, pulled herself up on the handrail and twirled herself right over. She did it again. I tried to do it, but I was nervous of not being able to get my feet back on the bridge.

'I can't do it,' I said.

'I'll help you.' She helped me twirl myself right over and put my feet back on the planks of the bridge.

'I'll have another go,' I said and twirled myself over. One of my feet missed the bridge and as the bridge was low my foot went into the water. I nearly lost my balance altogether and we fell about laughing at this. I lifted my foot which was dripping with slimy green water, causing another bout of giggles. Then we noticed a man coming towards us. Janet hauled herself up and over the handrail again.

'You're very good at that,' said the man who was now on the bridge with us. 'Show me how you do it.'

Janet did it again and he watched her. Her skirt flew over her head. I noticed her white cotton knickers. He said to me, 'Can you do it?'

'Only if she helps me.'

'Go on then, let her help you,' he said.

I looked at Janet and said, 'We've got to go home now.'

'Oh, that's a shame,' he said. 'Where do you live?'

'Not far,' I said. 'My mother's expecting us home, we've

got to go.'

'Have I upset you?' he said.

'No,' said Janet and we started to walk away from him. We broke into a run until we reached the edge of the field. We looked back at him standing at the edge of the copse of bushes.

'Look at him,' Janet said. 'The dirty bugger.'

He had undone his trousers and his big, pink dick was waving at us. We screamed with fear and laughter, and ran off before he could chase after us and catch us and do something terrible to us.

On Monday morning, Cathy sat next to me as usual on the bus going to school. She behaved as if she hadn't ignored me at Linda's party and asked me to go and meet her at her locker room after school so we could travel into town together to look at the shops. When I went to her locker room, I couldn't see her. I looked around at the tall tin lockers which were back to back in rows. The locker room was quiet, it seemed empty. I called her name. I heard giggling and movement. I walked round the locker room again. Cathy was there. I knew what she was doing. She was with someone else; they were hiding from me. It was possible for a slim girl to squeeze behind the lockers which were against the walls. There were pipes running around the walls at floor level and you could stand on these and move around behind the lockers.

'Cathy?' I said. 'Is that you?' More muffled giggling. 'Cathy, are you there?'

I felt hurt and had to swallow hard and choke back tears. I didn't know how to deal with this, so I left to catch the bus into town. I couldn't understand why she would treat me like that, but I had an idea it was about Roz. Cathy did not like me spending time with Roz. Gareth had told me that Cathy was besotted with Roz, and that the worst thing that happened to her was when Cathy got a scholarship to

Bolton School a year ahead of Roz and left their primary school. Cathy turned up at the bus station not long after me and acted as if nothing had happened.

'I went to your locker room and I couldn't find you,' I said. She shrugged her shoulders and smirked at me. We stood together silently until the bus came. When we boarded the bus, she sat next to me and started chatting. I was surprised at what she said.

'By the way, Gareth is going to ask you to go out with him,' she said. 'He's never had a girlfriend before, in fact he's never had many friends at all, with all the studying for Oxford. So, you will say yes, won't you? He enjoyed talking to you at the party.'

'I got drunk,' I said.

'I know,' she said.

As I write this, I have an idea that she was using this to have Roz to herself. She was manipulating me. If she hadn't said this, would I have started seeing Gareth? I don't know, maybe I would. I know I was naive and suggestible at that age. Cathy seemed much more streetwise than me. In fact, the whole family and all those three families who lived on that avenue seemed glamorous and fascinating, and I was dazzled by them.

It was Sunday afternoon. We were all in Roz's lounge having one of our music sessions. This involved sitting in a darkened room—the curtains had to be closed—while we drank endless cups of instant coffee, ate biscuits and listened to music. Roz and Cathy, and Roz's older brother, Keith, were sorting through the pile of records which we had all brought with us. *Jailhouse Rock* was playing. The volume was up high. Gareth and I were at the other side of the room sitting on the settee. We had been chatting, laughing about the party and me getting drunk on Babycham. He turned to me and put out his hand to touch my face. He stroked my cheek with his finger.

'Will you come to the pictures with me?' he said.

'It depends when it is,' I said. 'I can't go out during the week.'

'Can you go on Saturday?'

'Yes, probably,' I said feeling overwhelmed with embarrassment and anxiety and I didn't know what else.

'It's this,' he inclined his head.

'What?'

'Jailhouse Rock.'

This gave me a double problem. Mother would never approve of me having a boyfriend *and* going to see Elvis. Elvis 'the Pelvis' was shocking. The way he moved his body, the way he played his guitar, his hairstyle, his beautiful pouting lips, his rich voice and his American drawl were far too sensual and altogether too much for my parents. 'American rubbish,' my Father called it when a clip came on television one night. Bill Haley & His Comets had been bad enough, but they could laugh at that. Elvis took it to another level and that level was too overtly sexual, which couldn't be laughed at. He was common, said Mother. If they'd known the term 'white trash', they'd have used it. I had to say something about going to the cinema, so I lied and told Mother I was going with Cathy and Roz to the local fleapit in Tottington to see Elvis in *Jailhouse Rock*. She thought I was too young, but let me go when I said their mothers didn't mind.

I walked over to Gareth's house on Saturday afternoon, down the railway line as usual—there were no trains to watch out for on Saturdays. We caught the bus into Tottington and once we were in the cinema he headed for the back row. It was where all the courting couples sat paying hardly any attention to the film, just snogging the whole way through. The manager would patrol around with a torch from time to time and stop any activity that he thought was going too far. On this occasion, we mainly watched the film. Although I'd heard the LP of Elvis singing the soundtrack, I was unprepared for the impact of seeing him gyrate around on the screen. Elvis had a languid grace to him that was sexy. It was natural to him and his voice was a beautiful compliment to his body. To see him jive and sing the sequence to the music of the title song was a sensual delight to me at thirteen. I was turned on by Elvis and I wasn't much interested in Gareth's one or two attempts to kiss me. He smelled of tomato soup and neither of us knew what to do with our lips and mouths. It was awkward, but he was gentle and didn't try to devour me, which I'd heard boys sometimes tried to do. So, we did a sort of slightly open-mouthed lips-to-lips kiss but then he gave up when we bumped noses and we both laughed. He sat with his arm over the back of the seat resting on my shoulders for the rest of the film. I think he was as enthralled by Elvis as I was.

All the way home on the bus, we talked. He seemed very knowledgeable about all kinds of things. Politics, current affairs as well as his science subjects, although he didn't talk much about that. Trains, photographs and walking were his hobbies, different from mine, which were reading and playing tennis. I had to go straight home, so he walked with me down the railway line. When we reached the spot where I had to go through the broken fence, he stopped and faced me. He bent his head down and I lifted mine up. We had another kiss; this one was more successful, and he held me close to him. I liked the feel of his arms around me. He let me go and we smiled at each other. His eyes were clear grey.

'Will you come for a walk with me?' he said. 'Tomorrow afternoon?'

I nodded. 'That should be okay.'

'I hope it doesn't rain,' he said.

I ran the short distance home. No one asked me about the film; Mother was in the kitchen baking and Father was reading in the dining room, they were both quiet and seemed preoccupied with what they were doing. On Sunday I told Mother I was going over to see Roz in the afternoon, and I'd be home about five o'clock. She was not feeling well and went to lie down. It was a fine, mild day and I set off along the railway line feeling happy and wondering what this afternoon with Gareth would bring.

'Have you ever been up Holcombe Hill?' Gareth said as we set off back along the railway line. Holcombe Hill was facing us in the distance, appearing to be at the end of the railway line as we walked. It was omnipresent, visible as it was from both our houses, and had to be climbed.

'No, not yet,' I said. 'My father keeps saying we should go but we haven't.'

'It's my favourite walk,' said Gareth. 'It's quite steep in parts, will you be okay?'

'Yes, of course,' I laughed. 'I've got my flat school shoes on; I knew we were going for a walk.'

'The Peel Tower on the top was built in memory of Robert Peel, who founded the Police Force—he came from Bury. That's why they're called bobbies, after him,' said Gareth. 'We'll go up the railway line to the Hare and Hounds, and walk up the side of the pub.'

We arrived at the end of the line in the old station yard. There were several dilapidated wagons parked up in the sidings and weeds growing everywhere. On the side furthest from the main gates there was another place where the fencing was broken, and you could squeeze through overgrown shrubs. It came out behind some old cottages onto a dank and dark back alleyway. I shivered. The cottages and the alleyway seemed neglected and ancient. They had an eerie atmosphere. We crossed over the main road and walked up the steep cobbled lane at the side of the Hare and Hounds pub, which was the start of the climb up the hill. Trees and bushes overhung the track and made it dark.

'There's a sanatorium up here,' said Gareth. 'For people with tuberculosis.' We stopped and looked at the large stone building set in extensive grounds when we reached it. It looked like a stately home to me, not a hospital. Gareth said that was what it had originally been. 'The patients sleep outside on verandas for the fresh air,' he told me.

'I think I'd like to do that,' I said. 'It must be lovely all tucked up in bed, snug and warm but outside in the fresh air.'

Gareth laughed and took hold of my hand. His hand felt warm and firm. We walked hand in hand for a while until we came to a place where the path narrowed, and we had to walk in single file. We passed old stone cottages and farmhouses that looked as if they had been there for centuries as we climbed up and up. There were sheep in the fields on one side of the track boundaried by dry stone walls. We passed a few people coming back down as we approached the tower. I was surprised at the number of people on the hillside.

'It's everyone's favourite Sunday afternoon walk,' said Gareth.

The last part of the climb was steep until the ground flattened out where the tower was built. The stonework of the Peel Tower was black like all stonework at that time, due to air pollution from coal fires and mill chimneys. An open doorway was blocked by a heap of stone inside the tower. The tower was huge, much bigger than it looked from afar. We walked around it and looked out over the Pennine Hills, rocky, heather-covered moorland that undulated before us on each side. The tower was on the very top of the highest part of the hill.

'You can only go so far over there, it's an army training ground, on Holcombe Moor,' said Gareth, pointing. 'You can hear the guns sometimes.'

We looked around again, marvelling at the view. Gareth touched my cheek.

'Let's go back and have a cup of tea and a biscuit,' he said. 'And listen to some music.'

This outing set the scene for much of the time we spent together. Neither of us had a lot of money, we were dependent on our parents. We both loved exploring the countryside that lay on our doorsteps and we could both listen to pop music all day. So that's what we did: if it was fine, we would walk outside; if it was raining or cold, we stayed in Gareth's parents' front room and listened to music and perfected our snogging technique. Whenever we had any money, we would go to the cinema. He was hoping to pass his driving test soon and then we could go for drives in his mother's car.

Chapter 13
Lancaster 1861

The more I delve into nineteenth-century Lancaster, the more I realise that this is not just mine and my family's story, it's the narrative of the nineteenth century and the Industrial Revolution, of the movement of people—the workers—from country to town, from a rural-based agricultural economy to a town-based one, where dark satanic mills were built among those clouded hills, and where slums to house the workers packed in the unsuspecting farm labourers, who became weavers and spinners in the cotton mills. What hopes and ambitions were built into those massive mill buildings, the tall chimneys, the canals and later the railways. With every spadeful of earth dug up, with every brick laid, there was a vision of a future, an ambition and a hope for a better life. In this context does disappointment, loss and failure loom larger?

My mind is filled with Britannia Street and my ancestors. Elizabeth is the one I'm most interested in and I'm dreaming about her. I dream I'm in Britannia Street. My mother is there, she's holding a baby and she's crying. The baby is crying too. The baby sounds desperate but at the same time as if it has given up. Nobody is helping the baby. I want to take it from my mother and comfort it. I want to feed it and nurture it, but my mother holds onto the baby. I wake up crying. I am disturbed and unsettled by this dream. I feel unbearably sad and I know I must look for an explanation of this in Elizabeth's family. My life is quiet just now. My obsessive interest in Elizabeth has taken over. I can't do much else until I have understood her family situation. I make toast and coffee and, sitting at the kitchen table in my dressing gown, I open up my laptop and bring up the 1861 census.

Going back through time to the 1861 census and the family's earlier life, I find them in better circumstances than I found them in later years. A family whose father, William, is working as a clerk for the Ship Canal Company, and a family who could afford a live-in domestic servant, fifteen-year-old Ellen Townley. William Cock, my great-great-grandfather is thirty-five, and he is head of the family. His wife Esther, my great-great-grandmother is thirty-four. They live with their family of four children, Elizabeth, my great-grandmother, aged eight, Catherine, aged six, Christopher, aged two, and another Esther, the baby at six months old. Their address is Aldcliffe Street, Lancaster. The census form does not number or name the houses on Aldcliffe Street, so it's impossible to know which one they lived in. This address poses a problem as there is no Aldcliffe Street in Lancaster in the present day. I speak to Alicia, who looks in the A–Z and there isn't one listed. There isn't one on the map of old Lancaster that we have either. From the description of its position on the census return we suspect that it's now the road called Aldcliffe Road. If it is present-day Aldcliffe Road, then I am familiar with it, and I know that the houses are more substantial and of a much better quality than the Britannia Street homes. The houses on Aldcliffe Road are still there for one thing and are now desirable stone-built period properties, some detached and others semi-detached. The road connects directly to the town centre; it's on the front rather than being the back-street alleyways and courtyards that Britannia Street was. The family's future move to Britannia Street marks therefore a drastic change in their fortunes. This must have been brought about by William's death, some time in the ten years between 1861 and 1871. Two more children were also born between those dates.

There's something else nagging me … I'm sure there's something… Have I missed something? I look again at the listing on the census form and I notice that there is a gap of four years between the births of Catherine and Christopher.

There is a gap of two years or so between Elizabeth and Catherine, and the same between Christopher and baby Esther. I know from the 1871 census form that William followed Esther two years later and Mary Ellen came two years after that. Babies were born every two years in this family. I think this means there might have been another baby in this four-year gap. And I think that this baby might have died. In fact, I know this baby died.

I find the evidence on the ancestry website in the births and deaths. There was a baby born on 14th May 1857. He was christened John Robert and he died later that same year on 24th December. He was just seven months old when he died on Christmas Eve. What a tragic Christmas that must have been for all of them. Then, a few years later, Esther lost her husband and the children lost their father. This is heartbreaking. I send for birth and death certificates for all these events. I think I have found what I've been searching for, the story of what went wrong in Elizabeth's family. Baby John Robert's death was the start of it.

Some people hold the view that in the past the loss of a child, being more common, was not felt as deeply as we might feel it today. I don't believe that to be so. I'm sure this must have been a devastating experience, one of the worst things that can happen to anyone, no matter when they lived or how many children they had.

I am deeply saddened by this discovery, but I also have a sense of vindication. It vindicates my view that children are affected by changes in family fortunes and subsequent losses. It seems such an obvious thing to say, especially for a psychotherapist. I knew this before, but I know it now in a different way, at a deeper level of my being. Elizabeth's family disintegrated, a baby died, a husband and father died. My family also disintegrated. Not in the same way— although I don't know the whole story of Elizabeth's family, I'm sure there is more to discover. I feel that strange uncanny sense again. Is my life mirroring her life? Is she me? Am I her?

Chapter 14
Mother 1959

In the summer of 1959, Gareth and his family went away to their house in Wales for most of the holidays. He'd completed his A level exams and was ready for a break. He would be seventeen in October and I was thirteen. We stayed at home because Mother was ill and also because we had no money.

'Your father's going to have to get a job,' Mother said to me one day when we were in the kitchen eating our lunch of poached eggs on toast.

'What about the business?' I said.

'The business is losing money, we'll either have to put more money into it or fold it up,' she said. 'Your father wants to put money into it but there's... well, I won't agree to that.' Mother sawed into her toast with her knife and cut off a piece which she stabbed with her fork.

'What's going to happen then?' I said.

'Your father should get a job easily enough, probably in Manchester, but we can't move because of the problem with the house.'

'Oh,' I said. 'You mean the cracks?'

'Yes, they're getting worse all the time and Mr Hardcastle is just ignoring us.' Mother put down her knife and fork, leaving the rest of her toast uneaten. 'And I'm not well. I'm seeing Mr Harrison-Carter, the surgeon, next week so I'm hoping he'll suggest something for this pain in my back. The test results should be back by then.'

'Oh, right,' I said. 'I hope so too, err... by the way, you know Cathy?'

'Yes,' said Mother. 'Isn't she in Wales?'

'Yes,' I said.

'I think Roz is a much nicer girl,' said Mother, who by this time had met Cathy a few times and remembered one day on the bus back from Bolton when Cathy and I had walked behind Mother when we got off the bus. Cathy had made remarks and giggled, saying in a barely concealed whisper to me that Mother had a sexy walk. I didn't like it and neither did Mother.

'I know,' I said, 'but her brother, Gareth, is really nice.'

'Oh,' said Mother. 'Is he the one who's going to Oxford?'

'He's going next year, he's too young this year so he's staying on in the sixth form for a year.'

'How old is he?'

'Sixteen.'

'Sixteen? He must be clever.'

'He is, very clever and very nice.'

'Oh?' Mother stopped collecting the plates together and looked at me.

'Yes, well, he and I are friends… you don't mind, do you?'

'Is it him who's been writing to you?'

'Yes, from Wales.'

'You're too young for a boyfriend.'

'I knew you'd say that, but we just want to spend some time together, listening to music and maybe going to the cinema, you know, that sort of thing.'

'I suppose there's no harm in that. You can bring him for tea sometime, then I can meet him,' said Mother. She sighed and pushed the plates to one side. 'The painkillers make me tired; I think I'll have a lie-down for an hour or so.'

'I could do some ironing for you.'

'Will you? That would be a great help.'

Mother was often tired and in pain and needing to rest in the afternoons. To me she was old, most of my friends' parents were younger, but she was forty-seven at this time. Father was two years older than her. I would go to the tennis club or over to see Roz. We spent our time playing tennis or table tennis, or going to Bury and Chez Odette, or to Bolton and another coffee bar called the Casa Blanca. This one was Spanish themed, opened by a local woman who had lived in Spain, 'a land of garlic and greasy food',

Mother said. The décor was in a style completely new to us: brick walls were painted white, empty wine bottles encased in raffia hung on the walls, and wine bottles stood on the tables with candles stuck in them. The candle wax had been allowed to drip down the bottle and form a waterfall of wax. These two coffee bars, Casa and Chez, as we called them, were a new exotic species that had recently landed in our damp north-west corner of Britain. They were like birds of paradise sitting on starlings' nests. They brought a hint of exotic climes, of sunshine and warmth, of places where people sat outside and drank coffee and wine, and had a different way of life. How we loved them! They brightened up our lives in grey, post-War England.

Mother and Father still talked about 'the War', but that was gradually receding into the past. The air raid shelter that Grandad Cox had dug out for them in the garden of the old house was long gone and the area grassed over. Everyone said another war like those two World Wars would never happen again. A new world was dawning, anything could happen, there was a sense of being on the precipice of change. The old order was going. The two World Wars had forced change and we were about to leave behind the miserable, hypocritical 1950s. In Manchester there was Granada Television with its northern grittiness and working-class people, there was the rise of the 'kitchen sink' drama—*Look Back In Anger*, *A Taste Of Honey*, *Spring and Port Wine*, which was even set in Bolton. There were 'angry young men'. Fidel Castro became premier of Cuba, and there was Che Guevara, every teenage girl's dream hero. There was the Ban the Bomb campaign and the M1 motorway. There were supermarkets, there were more and more cars, and young men borrowed their parents' cars or even drove their own. There was pop music, there were coffee bars, there were Chinese restaurants. And there was sex. Of course, there'd always been sex, but there was a different attitude in our new generation, more open, less hypocritical. Deference was out, irreverence was in. We felt it even if we didn't articulate it, we knew it in our bones—it was a time of change. My generation were going to do things differently. I was going to do things differently. I didn't want a dull bourgeois life. I wanted excitement.

One day Mother and I were walking slowly—which was all she could do at this point—towards the shops at the end of the road when we saw, walking towards us, Mrs Hardcastle, the builder's wife. Mrs Hardcastle was like a caricature of a prosperous, northern businessman's wife. The sort you could imagine to be Lady Mayoress to her husband's Mr Northern Lord Mayor. She was small and fat and wore tailored suits and a hat. She gave off an air of pomposity and small-mindedness. She had a smug expression on her face, her small mouth pursed. She looked at us. I felt Mother's body tense. Mother looked at her, neither of them smiled or spoke. Mother turned her head away, snubbing Mrs Hardcastle completely. I didn't know what to do, should I acknowledge Mrs Hardcastle, or should I ignore her? I gave a little kind of halfway nod to her as Mother and I carried on walking right past her. I was shocked by this because it was so out of character for Mother to behave in that way. She was usually polite and friendly. I was linking her arm when this happened, and I felt her trembling as we walked on.

'I can't speak to that woman,' she said. 'They're playing for time, avoiding the problem, doing anything to get out of their responsibility for what's happened. It's their fault and they should put it right, but they don't answer our letters and it's all—so slow,' she said. 'It just grinds on and on, and your father has got enough on his plate, winding up the business and applying for jobs, trying to salvage something from the ruins of that and with me being ill—it's too much.'

'Let's go home,' I said.

I thought she was going to cry in the street. That was when I realised how much the problem of the cracks in the house was affecting my parents. We sat at the kitchen table with our tea and digestive biscuits, and Mother told me that

Father had a solicitor on the case now, and that we and Mr and Mrs Cornell next door were employing a specialist surveyor who would investigate the cause of the problem, which everyone thought lay in the foundations.

'But it all costs money and we haven't got any. We'd better win this case when it comes to court, if it ever does, but the solicitor can't do anything until this surveyor has been. So, we're waiting... we'll have to push him... and your father's not coping well, he keeps complaining of that pain in his side. It's his nerves again. And I... well, I've had enough of the whole lot... when I'm better, I think... I could get a job as a housekeeper.' She wiped away a tear that had fallen down her cheek and looked at me. 'You know, live-in somewhere, would you come with me?'

'I don't know, where to?'

'Wherever I can get a job, anywhere, somewhere well away from here, anywhere, I wish we'd never come here.'

'What about Father?' I said.

'He'll have to look after himself,' she said. Her face was sad, and her mouth turned down. Her fine grey hair was in need of a perm. She looked old and tired. I hadn't realised things were so bad. I felt sad to see her in this defeated frame of mind. Another feeling was creeping up on me; I was in a little boat which was slowly filling with water and drifting out to sea. I had no oars and I was powerless. I felt unsafe.

The following week, Father took Mother to see the consultant. He suggested some deep X-ray therapy to Mother's back. They came home saying that she had crumbling vertebrae, which the treatment should fix. Father took her in the Morris Minor for treatment at the Christie Hospital in Manchester. The treatment made Mother ill. She was sick all the way back, so next time they took a plastic bucket with them so she could throw up into that. I don't know how many of these treatments she had; it seemed to go on for weeks. It would involve most of the day and then Mother would go to bed for a day or two afterwards. Each time it took her a long time to recover from this treatment and the problems with her back were hardly improved at all.

Chapter 15
Life and Death 1851

Great-great-grandfather William Cock and Great-great-grandmother Esther Dickinson were married on 10th April 1852 in the parish church of Tatham, the Church of the Good Shepherd. Their marriage certificate records both as 'of full age', meaning they were over twenty-one. William's profession is bookkeeper. There is nothing under the heading of rank or profession for Esther. Her residence is listed as Wennington Bridge, and William's as Lancaster. William's father, my three-times-great grandfather is named as John Cock, schoolmaster. Esther's father is Robert Dickinson, yeoman. The witnesses are Thomas Carr and Margaret Cock, presumably William's sister or aunt. Robert Dickinson is not a farm labourer but a yeoman. This distinction implies he was a farmer with his own farm. And John Cock is a schoolmaster. I imagine that these two men with these occupations would mean that the status of their families in the villages where they were brought up, both small rural communities, would have been high. William and Esther must have seemed like a good match and there must have been every reason to expect a prosperous and happy future for them. I'm ridiculously pleased with this thought and I'm still marvelling at the power of these old records to move me to extremes of emotion.

The 1851 census shows William as a young man of twenty-five, single and working as a clerk in the Ship Canal Company office. He is lodging with Christopher Dickinson and his wife, Betty, in their house in the Ship Canal Company's yard, Canal Side, Lancaster. Christopher Dickinson is a joiner. Is he a relative of Esther Dickinson? If so, he may have introduced William and Esther. Twenty-three-year-old Esther is also living in Lancaster—in

Cheapside, one of the main shopping streets in the centre of the city. She is housekeeper to John Watson, aged thirty-eight, a draper, and his apprentice draper, Nathan Hutchinson, aged seventeen.

I am struck by the fact that William and Esther named their firstborn son John Robert, probably after each of his grandfathers. To be able to deduce that love and thought went into naming their son, who then died seven months later, is poignant. That the bare facts are starkly laid out in front of my eyes increases their power to affect me.

I'm waiting and watching for the envelopes from the Lancashire Registry Office. As soon as the post arrives, I rush to the front door. When I see the Preston postmark, I rip them open and scan the contents. Baby John Robert's death certificate arrives first. And what I see shocks me. The cause of death is 'chronic hydrocephalus'. I know a little about this, but I also look it up on the Web. Baby John Robert was born with a congenital birth defect in which part of the nervous system fails to develop normally. There are different degrees of this defect, the affected area is usually the lower back and may be evident as a kind of exposed sack. It can cause the cerebrospinal fluid, which normally circulates in the brain, to build up. In infants the skull enlarges quickly and causes pressure in the brain. This leads to symptoms including irritability, vomiting, difficulty in feeding and seizures. Babies with this condition typically have a high-pitched cry.

John Robert would have been an irritable, crying baby who must have suffered with this condition for all seven months of his short life. He must have been a difficult baby to care for if he had feeding problems and was constantly crying. I imagine Esther trying to feed him only to have him vomit afterwards. There were two other children to care for as well. It must have been hell. What a strain it must have been on the whole family, to see their firstborn son growing more grotesque in appearance as the weeks passed. He was dying before their eyes.

Nowadays, this condition can be treated with a shunt into a vein which drains the fluid from the brain continuously into a blood vessel in the child's body, so it is very unusual to see an infant with hydrocephalus, but I remember seeing it when I was a child before we moved to Holcombe Brook. There was a baby with a huge head in the neighbourhood where we lived. This baby was wheeled about in its pram, and Mother and I would encounter this child on trips to the shops. The child had the typical 'sunset eyes', the downturning of the eyes which occurs as the skull swells and pressure inside the head increases. I was equally fascinated and appalled by this deformed child when I was a little girl.

What this must have done to William and Esther and to their two little girls Elizabeth and Catherine, I can only begin to imagine. Such trauma and loss can damage families irrevocably. Their marriage, which must have started with hopes of children to bring them joy, now brought them such a tragedy early in their married life. William, working not in the mill or as a manual labourer of any kind, but as a clerk in the Ship Canal Company—what did this do his sense of who he was? A family doing well, rising in this world where possibilities for advancement may have seemed to be his entitlement. The birth of such a child could have injured his sense of who he was and Esther's too; things like this didn't happen to families like them. It could have felt like a terrible failure. It must have wounded both deeply. Did this contribute to William's death and the family's decline? I suspect it did.

This is the start of confirming what I already know. That something did go wrong in Elizabeth's family like it did in my mine. It also demonstrates that during eras like the 1960s and the 1800s, when rapid change occurred, how the outer world potentially influenced the inner world of the people who lived at that time and place. Those times when social mobility seemed more possible and there was hope that we could all have better lives. The Ship Canal

Company, the railways, the Industrial Revolution; it was all happening on William and Esther's doorstep. But personal, individual loss of all kinds can derail these aspirations and can bring down families, and individuals within these families. Great-grandmother Elizabeth was four when John Robert was born. She, as the eldest child, would have been aware that there were problems with her new baby brother and as time went on she must have picked up her parents' distress, sadness, anger, despair, whatever they felt and whatever they did to deal with the daily ordeal of a sick, irritable child whose skull was increasing in size and who they must have known would not survive. Elizabeth would have been about the same age as I was when I first saw the child with the huge head. It would have had a daily impact on her.

When baby John Robert did die, William and Esther and their children must have been in a turmoil of grief and mixed emotions. Relief at no longer having to try and comfort and feed him, but perhaps guilt at feeling this, and sadness and anger at the loss of him. Why had this happened to them? Did they do something wrong? It was the stiff upper lip approach to problems then and for a long time after, and I think this can only have contributed to a strong sense of shame. A successful young couple moving up in the world; a grossly deformed baby, their firstborn son—it's a tragedy and one that must have caused great damage to the whole family.

When I had my own first baby, my father told me that I myself was a crying baby for the first seven months of my life. I couldn't eat and failed to thrive, and it looked as if I might die. John Robert was a crying baby for seven months, albeit a seriously deformed and sick baby, who did die. I am fortunate that I survived, but those seven months must have been traumatic for my parents and for me—as an infant, never feeling the satisfaction of a digestible feed must have had a huge impact. This experience which was coupled with parents who kept their distance emotionally to lessen the

113

pain of any future loss must have affected me at a deep level of my development. Although an infant of that age does not have a conscious mind and memory, psychoanalytic theory considers that memories of early experiences are felt and stored as bodily experiences. These somatic memories are unconscious and may be played out in everyday life without our realising that this is what is happening. Modern science and technology can demonstrate through studying the brains of traumatised people, in a way that was not possible until recently, that what is played out unconsciously in the consulting room and in our everyday lives can have its basis in early traumatic experiences. The brain is changed as a result. I believe the attachment theory that suggests those early experiences made me fearful of being abandoned and unloved, hence my needing and wanting always to have a family around me. Once formed, I think I made attachments that were very strong. The house in Holcombe Brook, built on inadequate foundations—although this was very real—was a metaphor for my internal world. It chimed with my sense that I didn't have enough of a firm base within me to build on. It may have been even more terrifying on an unconscious level. I have always been longing and searching for a passion to fill that gap within me.

I have the birth certificates of all of Esther and William Cock's children in front of me and my heart stops when I look carefully at Elizabeth Margaret's. I can hardly believe what I'm seeing, written in the beautiful copperplate handwriting of the time. Her birth date. It's the eleventh of January, the same as mine. *We share the same birthday.* I shiver with shock. That cold finger from the past has touched me once more. What does this mean? Am I channelling her in some way? This is more than mere coincidence and I don't know what to make of it, but I am in awe at the strength of connections between the past and the present. More than ever I think I'm doing this research, writing this story for great-grandmother Elizabeth as well as for myself. And by writing down my own story as well as Elizabeth's, it gives me a different view on things, both literally and figuratively. Elizabeth and I both had to cope with life events at an early age which we weren't equipped to deal with.

The birth certificates are full of information. Elizabeth Margaret was born at 4 Aldcliffe Lane. Her father registered her birth a month later and gave his address as 4 Aldcliffe Lane, so there is no doubt that this was where the family was living. On the 1844 map of Lancaster, Aldcliffe Lane is the road that is now named Aldcliffe Road. John Robert's birth and death certificates both give his address as 4 Marston Street. This street is in the centre of Lancaster, right next to the church where Esther and William's daughters were married, and where the children were baptised. Catherine was also born in Marston Street. But Christopher Somerville Cock was born at Aldcliffe Street, in December 1858, so during the year after John Robert died, the family had moved from Marston Street. It looks likely that this house move was an attempt to leave behind the painful and unhappy associations the Marston Street house held for them concerning baby John Robert. Could it be that all the Aldcliffes—Road, Lane and Street—are the same place? It looks as if that might be the case as Aldcliffe Road is the only remaining Aldcliffe. The next child, Esther, was born at Aldcliffe Street in September 1860, as was William, in January 1863. Mary Ellen was born two years later in June 1865, in Britannia Street. So, the family moved to Britannia Street some time between 1863 and 1865.

William Cock's death certificate has also arrived. It has more tantalising clues as to what caused the family's downfall. William died on 19th November 1865, about five months after the birth of Mary Ellen. He was 39 years old. His occupation was given as bookkeeper and he died at home in Britannia Street, with his daughter Catherine Cock in attendance. The cause of death is given as 'chronic softening of the brain sometime serous apoplexy'. What does this mean? The word chronic denotes that the illness was of long standing. It is likely that William at some point could no longer work and that precipitated the move to Britannia Street. This must have been between the births of their son William, in January 1863, and their daughter Mary Ellen, in June 1865. They lost their domestic servant then, so Esther had six children to look after and a sick husband. So, what was this mysterious illness? Chronic softening of the brain implies organic disease. The diagnosis would have been made in those days by studying his history and symptomatology, considering any other factors that might cause such a change in the brain. Serous apoplexy could be describing fits or seizures caused by the brain disease. The word 'serous' is strange, does it mean serious? Or does it refer to some serous effusion on the brain? The copy of the death certificate is not a photocopy of the original, where the handwriting may have been difficult to decipher and when the word 'serous' or 'serious' could be open to interpretation. The copy has been typed and the word is unequivocally 'serous'. However, this could still have been an error in transcription and the original could have been written 'serious'. But whether serious or serous, the word apoplexy tells us that William had fits of some sort due to brain disease or damage. Was the doctor trying to be diplomatic? Was softening of the brain a euphemism for something too shameful to commit to paper?

Softening of the brain may mean an infection by a tumour or a stroke or perhaps some kind of dementia. Two other possibilities occur to me. One is syphilis, which in its later stages causes a condition called General Paralysis of the Insane (GPI), affecting the nervous system. The second is alcoholism, which can also affect the brain. Both were common at that time and I'm leaning towards alcoholism. Did William turn to alcohol to blot out his pain when John Robert was born deformed and subsequently died? So many questions form in my mind and there are no clear answers. I can only speculate, but whatever the cause, William was ill for some time, his behaviour may have been difficult and distressing, and Esther continued bearing children right up to the end. Did Elizabeth shoulder more of the burden than a twelve-year-old girl should have to? It's more than likely she did; she may even have had to work. Children did work in the mills at a very young age and there would be no money coming in if William couldn't work. Whatever the cause of William's illness, this must have been an extraordinarily difficult time for Esther. Maybe her own or William's family helped her in some way, but she was the one who had to deal with William's illness, while being pregnant with her sixth child, looking after the other children, losing her domestic help, moving from a spacious house on a good road to the Britannia Street slum and grieving the loss of a baby. When Mary Ellen was born, Esther's hands must have been full of childcare and domestic chores. Elizabeth as the eldest child would have had to help a great deal. With four young children and a baby, there must have been little time for anything else. Elizabeth must have witnessed her father's behaviour which, whatever the cause, if he was having fits would have been distressing. Seeing anyone have a seizure is disturbing—how much more so if you are a young child witnessing your father?

It was a rapid downfall. In a few short years, Esther's eldest son was born with a severe deformity and lived only a few months. Her husband became ill, was broken by his illness and died. The hopes and expectations that William carried for his family, as someone moving up the ladder of social mobility and success, died when he did. What was their source of income at that time? Whether they had savings, or Elizabeth worked outside the home, or family helped them, they would have been poor. It's a heartbreaking story and one that Elizabeth tried to leave behind when she came to Bolton. Or did she? Because my father knew some of this story. Someone told my father at least part of it. Was it Elizabeth? My father was supposed to be her favourite. Or did Great-aunt Annie or Grandad Albert Edward speak about it? There is no one left to ask now, they're all dead. I wish I'd asked more questions earlier.

William died, and Esther and her children survived. And Elizabeth brought this story with her when she later moved to Bolton. Some of it has been passed down the generations verbally. And it was carried unconsciously by Elizabeth's descendants, whatever they consciously knew. It's like a recording on a tape recorder—it cannot be seen but the tape has been changed; it's no longer blank. The sense and the feeling of it was and is in the very blood and bones of her descendants and influenced them in ways they probably knew not how. The previous generation mostly tried to rub it out, but I am grateful to my parents for having the courage to face it and tell me what they knew. Of course, the changing times helped, these things could be spoken of in the 1960s with a little less shame. But the past can never be entirely erased. It leaves a trace of what happened. It is a revelation to see the parallels in my own story: sick parents, loss of income, pregnancy before marriage—although I consider Elizabeth's family's downfall was much worse than mine. What would she make of it now? Discovering this story and writing about it helps me, it gives me confidence in myself. I feel it growing, I can look at myself and be compassionate. I am stronger for it.

Chapter 16
School 1959

Before the start of term in September 1959, I was sitting one evening in the dining room, reading. I had a new pile of books to devour which had been given to me by a friend of Father's who was retiring to a bungalow in Cleveleys. Why would anyone do that, I'd asked myself when I picked up the book. I couldn't think of one reason why they would want to live in a bungalow in Cleveleys. It was like being buried alive. But I was enjoying the books they had given me. Jinx was on my knee. Father was sitting opposite me, reading and sipping from a tumbler of whisky. His hand rested on the right of his abdomen. I knew this meant that the pain in his side was bad. We happened to glance up at each other at the same moment. Father smiled.

'Are you enjoying those books that Alfred gave you?' he said.

'I've just read a ghost story by Henry James, and this one is great,' I said. '*She*.' I held it up. 'By H Rider Haggard.'

'Ah yes, I'm glad you like them,' He seemed distracted. 'Beth...' he said and hesitated. 'There's something...' he cleared his throat. 'Something I must tell you—as you know your mother is having treatment... she's not well.'

'The treatment makes her ill,' I said.

'Well, yes, the treatment does make her ill, that's true,' he said. 'But there's something else and we're going to need your help, because...' He took a sip of whisky. 'Mummy might need an operation, on her back.'

'Won't this treatment make her better?'

'The consultant isn't sure, he wants to try it, but if it doesn't work then it will mean an operation.'

'Why didn't they just do an operation in the first place?' I said.

'Well, an operation is not without its dangers,' he said.

'And even if it's successful, there will be a long period of recovery, and I'm hoping to have a new job in September… when I've closed the business down and that means I won't be able to take time off to look after her… so, we're thinking that you might be able to do that.'

'Me? What about school?'

'I'll write to Miss Higginson, the Higg, that's what you all call her isn't it? I'll explain, it will only be for a week or two, do you think you could do that?'

'I think I could,' I said. 'I'd like to look after her.'

'Well, you'll be fourteen in January and Mummy said you can do the ironing and you can cook.'

'I won't miss school, I might miss my friends but not the work,' I said. 'And I hate having to get up so early since we moved here.'

'Oh, I didn't know you felt like that,' he said.

Gareth wrote to me regularly during the summer from Wales until he came home early in September the week before term started. The letters were partly telling me what he had done. The weather had been good, so the family took a picnic to the beach every day. They went sailing and had some days out visiting local beauty spots. It sounded as if they were enjoying themselves. Not for the first time I wished I had brothers and sisters to do things with. At the end of each letter he wrote about his feelings for me in an intense little paragraph. He wrote how he loved to kiss me and how my lips were like velvet. I was surprised and embarrassed by this, but I began to enjoy it when I got over my first reaction. He also made me laugh. He wrote that when they'd arrived, they found a weed growing up through the bedroom wall, they'd decided to call it a houseplant and left it there. They'd taken the two dogs and two rabbits with them. I wished I was with them, it sounded much livelier and more relaxed than anything I was used to.

At the start of term, I took a letter from my father to the Higg, the headmistress, explaining that I would have to take time off school to care for my mother. The Higg must have been in her forties at that time. She was a small, plumpish woman with short, permed, pale ginger hair swept off her face. She wore a dab of powder and lipstick, and her clothes were tending to the dark, smart and severe. She loved anyone who spoke 'nicely', and she decreed that we wore white gloves with our blazers and straw boaters in the summer. We were expected to conduct ourselves with decorum both in school and out. That meant no laughing or larking about on the streets of Bolton, and no eating ice creams while outside wearing our uniforms. It was the practice at that time that any letters to her from your parents, which were usually to explain why you'd been absent from school, were taken to her at break time in the morning. We formed an orderly queue outside her office (what else would we do?) and went in one at a time. It was a nerve-wracking experience even if you hadn't done anything wrong. I had a bad feeling about this letter as I suspected she wouldn't like it.

I took the letter in and stood in front of her desk while she read it. I looked around at her spacious office. There were signed watercolours on the walls and a lot of books on the tall bookcase. This room was a room belonging to a cultured and gracious person. The Higg looked up at me. There was no hint of warmth, no smiles, no commiserations.

'Do you know what your father has written to me about?'

'Yes, about staying off school to look after my mother,' I said.

'Isn't there anyone else?' Her voice was abrupt.

'I don't think so.' I felt my face burning with humiliation.

'What about your father?'

'He has to work.'

'I see,' she said. 'What about your schoolwork?'

I was silent, I didn't know what to say.

'I asked you a question.'

'I don't know,' I said. I was determined not to cry but I could hardly get the words out, I was so choked up. She looked at me again with that hard, cold look.

'I don't approve of this,' she said. 'Tell your form mistress and we'll send you work to do.' Her head went down, she wrote something. She looked up; I was still there. 'You may go.' She might as well have slapped my face hard. I was reeling and shivering.

I am angry as I look back on this. There was not one jot of concern about my mother, nor me except for the schoolwork situation. I understand that she didn't approve but a warm smile and a few kind words would have made all the difference. My disillusionment with school had started. It was known as the 'snob factory' in the town and I can understand why. It was a cruel place to be if you weren't performing well academically. You were a second-class citizen if you weren't Oxford or Cambridge material, and there was no understanding that family problems may be at the root of anyone not achieving their potential. It wouldn't have taken very much to get me on side. An understanding chat would have made a big difference. I realised that we weren't seen as individuals, although it was obvious that she had favourites who were usually posh, clever girls from posh, clever families. We were all dressed the same and were being processed in the same way towards high academic achievement, the pinnacle of which was Oxford and Cambridge. To me, from a family where no one had attended any university, the Oxbridge candidates at school seemed like remote bluestockings with whom I couldn't identify.

There was also, I see in hindsight, some poor teaching going on, although it was probably of its time. Many of the teachers were Oxbridge graduates who wafted about in their caps and gowns. Few had undertaken teacher training, it wasn't required. Most of them were single and there was only one male teacher. Favouritism was rife and obvious. I was interested in English and French, netball and tennis, art and drama. But the choices of which subjects you could take together were restricted and art was only possible if you could draw well. It was unimaginative. Later in life as an educator myself, I was determined to give my students a better experience.

A remarkable piece of poetic justice took place when I was in my forties and working as a freelance trainer. I taught counselling skills to teachers, nurses and others in the caring professions. I ran these courses for the health service and for groups within local authorities. At the end of one ten-week course, a course member approached me and asked me if I would be willing to run a course for some of the teachers at her school. They were thinking of setting up a pastoral service for their pupils. The school was Bolton School. In the late 1980s, they were finally thinking about their pupils' emotional welfare. Thirty years too late for me. I agreed, although I knew it would be hard to go back there and face the feelings I had about the place. But I did. My insides were churning, and I felt emotional as I parked my car and walked towards the mellow sandstone buildings. Inside, the polished parquet floors and heavy oak doors were familiar, reminders of my unhappiness there. Here was the senior dining room, the classrooms for Forms I, II and Remove. It is a beautiful building and I appreciated that when I returned more than I ever did when I was a pupil. But— deep breath in and out to calm myself—I had been given an opportunity to change that, to make my connection with Bolton School a better one.

The course ran for three days. It was a group of ten teachers, and once we had gone through the initial introductions I began to relax. They enjoyed it, it was a success, and I came out of it feeling pleased I had done something positive for them, and for myself in facing my own history connected with Bolton School. But I knew there was more to face. I had a strong sense that the past that I'd tried to leave behind was catching up with me.

Mother had an operation on her back. It was the removal of part of a disc in her spinal column. She was in a lot of pain, but she came home after one week in hospital.

There was a bed shortage and they discharged her early. I had stayed with Aunt Lizzy for the time she was in hospital and Gareth, who had now passed his driving test, dropped me off. We had a kiss and a cuddle at the back gate, and he left. Aunt Lizzy was disappointed she hadn't met him, but I was glad he hadn't been subjected to her scrutiny. As I look back, I see how vulnerable I was to anyone showing me affection and giving me cuddles. Although I knew that my parents loved me, they never said so and they never gave me cuddles or hugs or kisses. Father had been affectionate when I was little and although he was warm with me, he had stopped kisses and cuddles a long time ago.

It was a Saturday afternoon at the end of September 1959 when Mother came out of hospital. John had been up to see her while she was in hospital and stayed overnight with Father at the house. Mother said that neighbours had told her they hadn't opened the curtains in the morning, so the neighbours thought she had died. I didn't see John although I would have liked to. Father came to collect me from Aunt Lizzy's, and we stopped on the way at a supermarket that had recently opened. It was a new experience for both of us, helping ourselves to tins of baked beans and other groceries that were stacked in piles on the floor and shelves. I would have liked to linger and explore, but we needed to get back home to Mother.

Mother was in bed looking drawn and pale when Father and I arrived home. She managed only a weak smile when she saw me. I sat on the edge of the bed; Jinx was curled up beside her.

'Are you all right?' I said. 'Do you need anything?'

'I'll have a cup of tea if you're making one,' she said. 'I need to take my tablets, my back's hurting, and then I might have a little sleep.'

'Father got some chops for tea earlier,' I said. 'Will that be okay?'

'That's fine,' she said.

'I think I'll pop over to see Gareth,' I said. 'I'll be back in time to cook the chops.'

Mother nodded.

I darted under the broken bit of fencing onto the railway line and started a quick march over the sleepers. I still had that feeling of being on forbidden territory, and knowing I was walking down the railway line towards Gareth added to that. I was trespassing in all kinds of ways: I was too young, I shouldn't have a boyfriend, I should be concentrating on Mother, or doing my schoolwork and thinking about my future. I hadn't got the faintest idea about that. There didn't seem to be any careers advice at school or, if there was, I didn't know how to access it. Janet and I talked about it from time to time—neither of us wanted to do anything that involved much studying, nor did we want to be teachers. The choices seemed to be limited if you weren't going to Oxbridge. There were other universities, but it seemed like something that other people did. Teaching, nursing, secretarial, that was about it. Janet said nursing was just shovelling shit and she didn't want to be a student, so she thought she'd do radiography. It was a negative way of looking at it. Nothing was calling to me, I didn't know what was out there in the world. Nothing grabbed my interest apart from Gareth, pop music and the latest fashion. My horizons were limited. Looking back, I see I was at a turning point. Could a caring intervention from a teacher have changed the course of my life? Perhaps, perhaps not. School had already got me down as not interested in academia. My parents were too caught up with their health and ongoing legal problems with the house. I was on my own, drifting in that leaky boat through a choppy sea.

I'd not seen Gareth for a week. We saw each other usually on Friday evenings, Saturday afternoon and evening, and Sunday during the day. I fitted in our time between my jobs at home and no one seemed to notice. We tried to wangle an evening during the week too, usually a Wednesday when we might go to an early film showing, so it meant I wasn't home too late because of getting up early for school the next day. But now, I thought as I approached Gareth's front door, I wouldn't have to get up so early as I didn't have to make that loathsome long journey to school every morning.

Gareth whisked me into the front room, and we sat in our usual place on the sofa with music playing.

'Russell's still around,' Gareth said. 'He might come in here; he uses that little table as a desk when he's home from Oxford. If he needs to use the room, I'll show you how I develop my photographs.'

'Okay,' I said.

'Tessa's got a boyfriend, he's in the upper sixth with me,' he said. 'He's called Phil.'

'Is he a friend of yours?'

'I haven't got any friends, what with studying and being moved up first one year and then again, I'm the odd one out, they're all so much older than I am,' he said.

'Oh, that's awful,' I said.

'Well, you know…' he said. 'Anyway… Phil.'

'How long has she been going out with him?'

'A few months, I think, she didn't say anything for a while, we thought she was just going to the pictures with her old girlfriends from school, but anyway it was Phil.'

'Is he nice?'

'He's okay,' he said. 'Actually, I was a bit worried about her. We had a long talk when we were on holiday, and she said they'd slept together, only once, but they hadn't taken any precautions. I told her to tell him to buy some johnnies from a chemist's shop. Then she said she wasn't going to do it with him any more.'

'She could get pregnant,' I said.

'Precisely,' he said. 'Hey, listen to this, it's really funny.'

'Does your chewing gum lose its flavour (on the bedpost overnight?)' was playing over the music system.

'Do you ever put your chewing gum on the bedpost overnight?' I said laughing. 'It would never occur to me to do that.'

'Me neither,' he laughed. 'Who thinks these songs up?'

'Lonnie Donegan?' I said. 'Or whoever wrote it.'

'Yeah, probably, it's him singing it,' Gareth said.

Gareth leaned over and kissed me. It was a long one and he caressed me gently with his hand at the same time. He'd done this before but this time he put his hand up my jumper and manoeuvred it into my bra. I didn't stop him. He stopped and looked at me.

'You don't mind?'

'No, I don't mind, I just hope that Russell doesn't come in at the wrong moment.'

'Well, we just stop, that's all,' said Gareth.

'Hasn't he got a girlfriend?' I said.

'Not that I know of,' said Gareth. 'Actually, he became religious since he went to Oxford.'

'How come?'

'Well, my mother's a Catholic, so we were all baptised as Catholics, but we don't go to church. Mother goes occasionally but no one else does. I think Russell was lost when he went to Oxford, and he started going to church with a friend and that was it, he's religious now.'

'I wonder if you'll become religious when you go,' I said.

Father had a job in Manchester. He worked at J & J Shaw's as a carpet and curtain salesman. The J & J Shaw building in front of Oxford Road train station was to become familiar to me much later in life when I moved to south Manchester. When the shop closed, the building became the Cornerhouse, an arts cinema, which was to become an iconic Manchester institution. Working in Manchester meant an early start for Father. My job was to take a bowl of water to Mother in the morning, so she could have a quick wash before the district nurse came to change the dressing on her back. I made tea and toast for her breakfast, which we ate together in her bedroom. Then we planned the evening meal and I did any shopping that was needed. My father attended to the Aga, riddling the embers and filling it up, morning and evening, with anthracite. I cleaned the grates and laid the fires ready for lighting later if it was cold. I hoovered and dusted every other day. My mother's youngest sister, Aunt Helen, had recently moved to Bury, and she came every week to take the washing. She returned it all neatly ironed the following week. She worked full-time, had two young sons and looked after her mother (my granny, who was in her eighties), so she couldn't do anything more to help. Mother had two older sisters and two older brothers who all lived in Salford. We didn't see them often and they couldn't be expected to help. Her youngest brother lived in Bristol. Mother said I was good at looking after her, and both Mother and Father liked my cooking, which Mother taught me. The homework I was supposed to have been sent from school never materialised and no one thought to ring and remind them about it. I didn't miss school at all, although I missed Janet and my other friends, but I saw Gareth regularly and Roz sometimes. I didn't miss Cathy, in fact I avoided her whenever possible. I enjoyed that time at home.

Mother was improving and there was no need for me to stay off school any longer. I had been absent for four weeks, but my time off might as well have been a year, because it changed things and it changed me. When I returned to school, reluctantly, no one asked me how things were at home. I'd spoken to Janet on the phone a few times while I was off looking after Mother and I'd found it difficult. She was still my best friend, but she and my other friends had all carried on without me. They'd all put their names down to go youth hostelling for a few days in the Lake District with our form teacher and form prefect. I had never been asked and when I did enquire about joining them, I was told it was too late. They were all mates together and I felt hurt and left out. They had moved on without me. I didn't feel as if I fitted in any more.

As far as schoolwork was concerned, I didn't seem to have missed much, but I hated getting up and going out early in the morning, catching buses then sitting all day listening to teachers talking about equations, declining Latin verbs, deciding what kind of clauses a sentence comprised of or going around the class to have passages read out loud. Occasionally that was funny when someone who stumbled and stuttered over reading and mispronounced a word or misread a sentence. Others droned on as they read, especially Shakespeare when they didn't understand what they were reading—'out damn spot' mumbled in a monotone made us laugh and the teacher impatient. But it was cruel and caused suffering, no one had heard of dyslexia, and those who stumbled and stuttered were often humiliated. Why didn't someone recommend some good books to read? I'd exhausted the supply at home, we weren't near a library, and I had no idea, apart from the classics, which authors to choose. The only subjects I liked were cookery, needlework and games. Science, doing experiments, history, English and French weren't bad; geography and maths, I hated. I was bored and wanted to leave. I was there under sufferance and I began to behave badly. Well, badly for Bolton School. I would answer teachers back, forget homework, wear make-up and nail varnish, talk in lessons, sit on the back row whenever possible, chew gum and once or twice bunk off sports to go home early. My protest wasn't much at all, but for that school, in those days, it was bad. It was noticed. I was beginning to get a reputation as a bad girl. But I didn't care, none of it was important to me. I was marking time, both at school and at home. I was impatient to be free; I couldn't wait much longer.

'Beth, come in here a minute, I've something to tell you,' Mother called to me from the kitchen as soon as I closed the front door one day after school.

I went to stand with my back to the Aga. I leant against the rail and put my stockinged feet on the oven, one at a time, to warm them up. Jinx was in her usual position on her blanket. She stretched and yawned when she saw me.

'The surveyor's finally been today,' said Mother. 'He

looked at the cracks and said there's something seriously wrong, the cracks are not normal settlement, so he's going to come back and dig down under the house to look at the foundations.'

'Oh right,' I said. 'When's he doing that?'

'Soon, I hope,' said Mother. 'Those damp patches in the front room where the rain gets in are getting bigger and that crack near the window is getting wider.'

'I know,' I said. 'I hope he finds out what's wrong.'

'I think he will,' said Mother. 'Then we can have it put right and have the house decorated again.'

Chapter 17
Melling 1841

I'm nearing the end of the online documents. When I've exhausted the online searches, I shall visit the places where my family lived. The excitement of the search and the feelings about these long dead people are just as strong as they were when I first started this venture. To visit the places where they lived and to walk in their footsteps will be a charged experience. But first I'm searching for the 1841 census, which was the first one in Great Britain to list individuals. I find it easily. The original document, copied and available to see on the Internet, looks very old and has faded in parts. Great-great-grandfather William's place of birth is consistently recorded as Tatham on all the documents relating to him. The area of Tatham and Tatham Fell is a remote and sparsely populated parish in South Lakeland. Today it's a sleepy backwater, the landscape dotted with ancient farmhouses and cottages. It's not on the popular tourist routes of the Lake District. In 1841 with transport either horse-powered or on foot, it must have felt even more remote. At some point in the nineteenth century, the railway came to the area, but it didn't survive for long—Dr Beeching's infamous cuts in the 1960s included the Melling line.

Melling village is part of Tatham, a parish eleven miles from Lancaster. It's where Great-great-grandfather William and his family were living in 1841. It was recorded on the census forms along with Wrayton, the hamlet next to it, and all together there were nearly two hundred souls living there. Judging by the occupations of the inhabitants, it was a busy and lively place in the middle of the nineteenth century. Farming was the main occupation. Farmers who had their own land and property put down the acreage they owned and sometimes the number of people they employed on the census form. So, a 'farmer of seventeen acres', or 'farmer of ninety acres', or 'farmer of means,' or 'employer of ten' was how they described themselves. Women and children were all described in relation to the man of the house, farmer's wife, farmer's daughter. A house called Crow Trees was occupied by a 'landed proprietor'. There was the Vicar, the aptly named Reverend John Tatham. A blacksmith and his apprentice lived in Smithy House. There were two basket-makers, a shoemaker and several agricultural labourers, a carpenter, a dressmaker, a mason, a bead-maker, a tailor and a tailor's apprentice. There was a butcher, and an innkeeper, who ran the Horse and Groom public house.

In the centre of the village was Melling Hall, near the church. In 1841, it was the home of the local magistrate, his wife and son, and several servants: a housekeeper, a coachman, a lady's maid and five others. Living next door in Wrayton were two gamekeepers, who must have been part of Melling Hall and its estate. Across the road are the church and the vicarage. In the garden of the vicarage there are the remains of an old motte-and-bailey castle.

In the schoolhouse, living with his wife Anne and their four children, was John Cock, the village schoolmaster. Their children were fifteen-year-old William, Robert, thirteen, and Margaret and Catherine, aged eleven and eight. John Cock is my great-great-great-grandfather. This sets me off on a frantic search for more information about John, and what I find is remarkable. He was born into a family of agricultural labourers in 1794 and worked as an agricultural labourer and a collier before that. How did he make the transition from those humble occupations to schoolmaster? And where did he work as a collier? Were there coal mines in the area?

I discover that in those days there were many small privately owned coal mines around Melling—I found that someone called P J Hodson researched the area for his PhD thesis and published a book. Nowadays the remains of these are best seen by walking the fields. My research tells me that there are fenced-off holes in the ground, ruins and shafts in the middle of various fields, and the remains of an engine house in a field on Clintsfield Farm. All are on farmer's land. Many mines belonged to the Hornby Castle estate, and possibly still do. One man supposedly had his own coal mine under his house at Blands Farm. He would go down through a trapdoor from his kitchen to his cellar and retrieve as much coal as he needed for his fires. For a while, I'm taken off track to explore these fascinating discoveries further. It doesn't explain why John Cock became the village schoolmaster, but my reading has shown me that there were many accidents at these small coal mines, and men were killed and injured regularly. Earlier in his life, John Cock is variously listed on his children's baptism records as working as a farm labourer or collier. At this time, he lived at Millhouses, a hamlet in Tatham parish. People who buy houses there today are advised to search for evidence of mining. Is it too far a flight of fancy to imagine that if John Cock was injured and unable to continue physical labour, he was given the post of village schoolmaster?

But how could a boy from such humble beginnings be considered suitable for such a role? In 1841, there would be little or no teacher training, the schoolmaster would be appointed by the church, and probably there were few candidates for the post in such a remote place where agriculture was the main occupation. Could the vicar, the Reverend Tatham, have recommended John as a suitable candidate, possessing the qualities and the learning necessary to teach children? Maybe John Cock had been an unusually gifted pupil. I notice that in 1824 he named his second son Robert Byron Cock. Robert Byron was born in the same year that Lord Byron—the poet, romantic and revolutionary figure who enjoyed celebrity status—died at the age of thirty-six, fighting in the Greek War of Independence. Does this indicate John's love of poetry? I can only speculate. In any case, John must have been considered able to do the job. I feel a twinge of pride in John's abilities.

This move from his farm labourer and manual worker heritage to an occupation with higher status is shown to be possible. It may have engendered high hopes for John's children, especially the two boys, Robert and William. Girls were, of course, expected to marry, have children and look after their families. William did go on to become a clerk, so he moved beyond the unskilled labourer status. But his downfall was catastrophic. I am convinced that the loss of his son, John Robert, born deformed and suffering an early death, was connected to his downfall. William became ill and died at a young age. The family suffered with him. The sense of shame would have been huge. I don't think this is overstating the case. If anything, these things in the past have been *under*stated. The individual has been blamed. Now we understand the outside influences of culture, family and the time in which these events occurred. The individual's own psychology interacts with these external influences in each person's individual way. William was at the mercy of some of these external forces as well as his own psychopathology, all of which must have contributed to his own and his family's downfall.

Chapter 18
Gareth 1960

Gareth and I were in our usual place in his front room. It was a Saturday afternoon in March and everyone else was out.

'I'd like to show you my bedroom—is that okay?' he said to me as we drank our instant coffee.

'Yes, if you like, I've been past it when I've been to the toilet,' I said.

'It's very small,' he said.

'So is mine,' I said. 'And freezing cold.'

'Come on.' He grabbed hold of my hand and stood up. I followed him up the stairs and to the doorway of his room. He leant against the door and pulled me to him. Our kisses were practised now, gentle, luscious and arousing. His hand caressed my breast. I could feel him hard against me and I touched him.

'Let's lie on the bed,' he said.

We arranged ourselves so we could comfortably kiss and caress each other. His hand went up my skirt. I didn't stop him. Our lovemaking had slowly progressed from snogging—kissing and caressing—to what everyone called heavy petting, further exploration of each other's bodies. We were relaxed and familiar with each other. He talked to me without restraint about his body and how he responded to me. He had awakened my response with his touch, but neither he nor I knew much about my own response or female responses in general. What I did know was that we were only a tiny step away from doing 'it'.

'I think it's time,' he whispered in my ear, 'for us to go further.'

'What now?' I said.

'No, well yes, I would like to do it now, as you can tell,'

he said laughing. 'But I've thought of a special place for our first time.'

'I'm scared of getting pregnant.'

'Don't worry,' he said. 'I won't let that happen, I'll get some johnnies and we'll plan it, so we won't be disturbed, and it'll be special.'

A week later we lay sprawled out on the leather upholstery on the back seat of his father's Rolls-Royce, which was in the garage. The car was an old model, but nevertheless it was a Rolls-Royce. I looked up at Gareth's familiar face, his clear grey eyes, his lips slightly parted. He kissed me. I pulled away.

'Are you sure no one will come home early and find us here?' I said.

'Look,' he said. 'My father's at work and my mother's gone to the market, she'll be there all afternoon, Tessa and Cathy have gone to the cinema, there's really nothing to worry about at all.'

'As long as you're sure.'

'I'm sure,' he kissed me gently on the cheek. 'Don't you want to?'

'Yes, I do want to, I suppose I'm nervous, I don't know exactly why… you've got the johnnies, haven't you?'

'Yes, of course, but I wondered…' he looked at me.

'What?'

'I just want to feel what it's like without one for our first time—don't worry, I promise I'll be careful; I'll get off at Bury, I won't go all the way to Manchester.'

'Are you sure you can do that?' I said, giggling.

'Yeah, I'll do it, don't worry.'

So that was how it happened. It certainly didn't hurt as I'd read it might, the 'heavy petting' we'd been up to had prepared the way. It was over very quickly.

'Oh,' he breathed. 'Oh.'

He pulled away and that was that. He used his handkerchief to mop up. He lay half flopped on top of me and half falling off the seat.

'Well,' he said, giving me a small kiss. 'You are lovely and that was everything I thought it would be, but not easy to get off at Bury…'

'You're squashing my leg,' I said. He moved away. I wanted to get out of the car, I was still scared that someone might find us there. 'Let's go back in and have a coffee.'

I had to go home early as we were expecting my parents' friends for tea. They were the ones who had given me the books, so Mother had said I had to be there. I walked back along the railway thinking about what had happened. I had half expected that I would feel different somehow, but I didn't, except of course I knew a line had been crossed and I could never go back. I wondered what I had let myself in for, and I worried about getting pregnant. I'd read that sperm can swim up you from the outside and you can get pregnant like that. Gareth was due to start at Oxford in the autumn; before that he would be going on family holidays with his parents. A break might be good for us. Maybe Mother was right, he was a bit intense. But I knew I was going to miss him. Suddenly a tremendous noise broke through my thoughts… I felt a massive presence behind me. I turned, and the train, the great, steaming black mass of it was behind me, advancing at speed. I threw myself off the track onto the grass at the side and lay there shaking. How could I have not seen or heard the train? I could have been killed. I sat for a while on the grassy bank at the side of the track and watched the train steam away. I cried as I thought about what could have happened. I must be more careful.

Gareth and I were spending nearly all our spare time together. I had hardly any time to see Roz and Janet. Gareth was good at finding places and opportunities for us to be alone. I went along with it, not always sure whether I should. But I loved him and trusted him, and it wasn't that I didn't want to do it, but rather that it was me who seemed to be the one worrying about being found out or getting pregnant. What a scandal we would make if anything did go wrong. When he went on holiday with his family to Wales at Easter, I could think of little else but Gareth and our lovemaking, because he rang me every other day and wrote passionate letters to me. Almost every day there was a letter. I was shocked by the detail he put into them. So shocked that now I can't remember or even imagine anything that was approximately like what he wrote. My mind can't do it. I knew he shouldn't write like that, such explicit details of our lovemaking. I tried to write back in a similar vein, but I couldn't bring myself to write like he did. After I sent one or two of these attempts, I abandoned this and told him he should burn my letters. I kept his in my room in a drawer, I don't know why. I wrote his name on my ruler and adorned it with hearts. I told Janet what we were doing, but no one else knew. It was a secret.

Mother had recovered from her operation, but she was still unwell, still suffering from back pain, although the operation had provided some relief. There were things she found difficult or impossible, the piano was sold as she could no longer play due to problems with her arm on the side of the mastectomy. She couldn't walk far, but she could sew, and she made some loose covers for Roz's mother and for the Browns. She started going to church—C of E this time—in Tottington, on the other side of Greenmount. Father still had the pain in his side and sat most evenings with his hand on his abdomen, nursing it. He had hospital appointments and tests and investigations, all of which showed nothing physical; he had a spastic colon, the doctor said, caused by worry, and he was on mild tranquillisers. Mother had told me he'd lost almost all the money he'd invested in the business in Accrington. But they were trying to be positive, looking forward to the house situation being resolved when they should have enough money to fulfil their long-term ambition to buy a bungalow in Kent. It would be a complete change, a nicer place to live, and it would be easier for them to manage. They were waiting for the surveyor's report on both our house and next door's. The surveyor had told them verbally that there were definite problems with the foundations. They were inadequate to support our house due to it being built in a place where there had been a pond. The house was sinking and falling to one side and pulling the house next door with it. It looked like we had a case against Mr Hardcastle.

I came home from school in the middle of the summer term to find my mother upstairs lying on her bed. This was unusual as she had been managing without a rest in the afternoons for a few weeks now. I went up and found her crying, facing the wall with her back to me.

'What's the matter? What's wrong?' I said scanning through things in my mind as to what it could be: her health, the house cracks, Father, John. She didn't turn to look at me but thrust her hand out behind her. I saw she had a fist full of Gareth's letters. I ran out of the room and down to the telephone in the hallway. I dialled Gareth's number. He answered. My mouth was dry. I could only just articulate the words.

'You've got to come over, my mother's read your letters.'

My mother couldn't speak about it and that was all I could say to Gareth. I was in a strange state. Where should I go? What should I do? I went to my bedroom pacing the square yard of carpet that amounted to paceable space. Then I sat on the bed. Then I lay on the bed. I paced again. This was something too shameful, too awful to speak about, I could hardly dare to think about it. The rest of what happened that evening or afternoon is not very clear. All I remember is being scared and full of shame. At some point, Gareth arrived at our house, and my father arrived home. He took Gareth into the front room to speak to him alone. Gareth came out crying. I was shocked to see him cry. I'd never seen him cry before. I was disappointed in him. He shouldn't have cried. Gareth had to go home, my father would be going to see his father and we were forbidden to see each other again. One minute, my father said, 'You've done something your mother never did at your age,' then the next minute: 'I suppose not everyone gets asked.'

The letters, the terrible, shameful letters had been left by me on a chair in my bedroom that morning, after I had been searching for something in the drawer where I kept them. I knew I'd left them there, I noticed them before I left that morning for school. Usually I put them away, out of sight, but I remember thinking that I could trust Mother not to read them. But I had *chosen* to leave them there. Ever since, I've wondered if part of me wanted her to find them. I think the answer must be yes, I did. Then Father read them too and put them in his desk drawer and locked it. I wanted to disappear with the thought that they'd both read those excruciating letters. Father said they were to be kept as evidence in case they were needed in the future. What we had done was against the law. Gareth had broken the law. I was underage and he wasn't, so he was responsible, and he could be prosecuted if my father chose to do so. I suppose I vaguely knew this and I'm sure Gareth knew it.

Father went to see Gareth's father. Our mothers spoke together. Mrs Evans said she knew we were alone together a great deal, but she thought we were too young to be doing anything like this. No action was to be taken at that moment but, if necessary, I would be made a ward of court. Father explained this to me and said it was for my own protection and if Gareth came near me, he would be in serious trouble. We didn't speak much to each other, Mother, Father and I, except to say, 'Pass the salt please.' The weight of this awful thing pressed down on all of us and we couldn't put it aside. I could hardly look at them, I was so ashamed and humiliated. I went to school and carried on as normal. I told no one. I missed Gareth but I was also relieved that I didn't have to worry every month about whether I would start my period. Mother, Father and I were all in a sad and distressed state of mind, and it was all my fault. Mother lay down in her bedroom a lot and Father sat with his hand on his abdomen a lot. I stayed in my room. I did my homework there and went to bed early and was off early to school. As if they hadn't got enough troubles without me adding to them. We could hardly look each other in the eye. I cried one night in bed for a long time. Mother came into my room. She sat on the bed in the dark.

'I expect you feel that you've let us down?' she said.

'Yes,' I whimpered. Mother sat there with me for a while. She smoothed my hair and kissed me before she left. I was comforted by this and I wished she'd done more of that sort of thing before. I woke up early crying again. I was a bad person to have gone along with Gareth and I had hurt my parents.

What came as a great relief to my parents and a shock to Gareth and Cathy, as relayed to me by Roz, was the news that Gareth's family were to move away. They were going to live in Wales; his father was taking early retirement due his ill health. His heart was weak, and he had a bad chest. They were leaving in the summer holidays. So, with Gareth away at Oxford and his family living in Wales, he and I would be far apart.

I carried on without Gareth, but felt a great gap in my life. At the same time there was a lightness in me without the continual nagging worry about pregnancy. So, I went to school, there was nothing else to do. But school held even less interest for me now. I was determined to leave at the earliest opportunity. Janet and one or two other friends kept me going when I was there, although Janet had moved to a new house to live nearer to school and went home at lunchtimes. I was lonely without her. I had a small, select handful of friends and I didn't mix much with the others. I teamed up with Roz at weekends and holidays as she also, conveniently for me, had lost her best friend Cathy, due to the move. It's a tricky thing, this managing of female friendships and boyfriends. Gareth had not given me the space to do much with my girlfriends, but Roz never mentioned that. I filled a gap for her too, and we carried on where we had left off. Tennis would start again in the spring. Shopping, listening to pop music, and experimenting with clothes and make-up was all year round. We became more sophisticated, and our clothes and our make-up made us look older than we were. We were both taken out by a series of boyfriends. Some were friends of the Browns, some came into the coffee bars we frequented, some were from the tennis club, and some were schoolboys. We were less interested in the schoolboys as they were young and naive, and without money or a car to drive so they couldn't take us anywhere interesting.

I hung about with the tennis club crowd for a while and one of them attached himself to me in a casual kind of way. He wanted to be my boyfriend, but I kept him at arm's length. That came to a sudden end one evening. The tennis club was open all year round and I was in the clubhouse where a few of us had gathered and ended up playing table tennis. I was partnered by Gary, the wannabe boyfriend, playing against Dave and Andy. Gradually people left until it was just the four of us when the game ended. I put down my bat and went to sit on a bench. The three boys came towards me. No one spoke. An unnerving tenseness filled the space between us as they surrounded me. I stood up and put up my hands.

'No, no, leave me alone.' I tried to dart between them but there were three of them, strong, tennis-playing, young men aged seventeen and eighteen. I was a slender, fourteen-year-old girl of five foot two inches. They grabbed me and began to pull off my shirt, my jeans and then my bra. I struggled, but it was hopeless. All that was left were my pants.

'No, please,' I begged and sobbed. 'I've got my period, you don't want to see that, please, please leave me.' And they did. I grabbed my clothes, took them into the women's changing room, locked the door and got dressed. Should I try and climb out of the lavatory window? No, it was too small. I'd have to dash out of the room and hope for the best. I looked round the door, the three of them were sitting chatting with cups of coffee in their hands. I ran out of the changing room and out of the clubhouse and never went back there alone.

The Browns' friends worked, mostly in their fathers' successful businesses, and had cars and money. They paid for drinks in pubs where we were never questioned about our ages, and we learned to drink gin and tonic, and port and lemonade. They took us to clubs in Manchester, where we loved to dance. Roz and I were great dancers, having perfected our technique with plenty of practice at home during the weekends. None of the boys were as good as we were. These clubs—the 3 Js (our favourite), the Expresso Bongo and the Copacabana—were dark, noisy places. The music and dancing were the thing, drinks were expensive and there wasn't much chance of a conversation above the loud music; shouting and sign language were the ways to communicate. If I'm honest, I knew this wasn't really my scene, but there didn't seem to be much else to do. There was always some snogging at the end of these evenings in a lay-by or some farm track on the way home, but I never wanted to go any further. None of these boys were for me.

After a few months, though, both Roz and I found ourselves with boyfriends. I met mine in Chez, and we got talking. Patrick was from an Irish Catholic family and his father was a local doctor. Patrick was at a crammer in Manchester to improve his A levels so he could go to medical school. He seemed half-hearted about this, and as I was whole-heartedly negative about my own education, we had this in common. Our romance was conducted with the usual round of cinema-going and sitting in Chez. He told me about his family and the Roman Catholic religion, which I knew nothing about. He'd been to boarding school in Ireland, and he told me about Irish history and the English, about which I was also ignorant. The history at school was about long dead kings and queens. I had enjoyed the story of Queen Elizabeth I and Mary Queen of Scots, but I wanted to know about ordinary people and how they lived, and about the rest of the world. I wanted to learn about art and its history, I wanted to visit art galleries and be able to discuss the art with someone knowledgeable. I wanted to learn more about classical music and about how the political system worked and the religions of the world. Father was usually a good source of information, but he was not much in the mood for talking these days. My eyes were slowly being opened to what was withheld from me—what I wasn't learning. I was bored and frustrated at school and beginning to see that although I was supposed to have received a good education at the 'snob factory', in fact it was limited.

Things were warming up between Patrick and me after a few weeks of cinema and Chez and walks around Bury town centre. One day I got off the bus from school and I noticed a man draw up his car alongside me. I tried to hurry along and move away, thinking he was another weirdo, but his passenger window was wound down and he leaned over to speak to me.

'You're Beth, aren't you?' he said. 'I'm Patrick's father, I've just come to tell you that Patrick can't see you any more, he's got to concentrate on his A levels, he's going to go to university, do you understand?'

I stared at him; I couldn't believe what had happened. I partly wanted to defy him and see Patrick anyway, but I didn't want any more trouble. I didn't really know what I wanted, but certainly no more trouble of the parental kind that involved boyfriends. I could see endless trouble ahead with my Englishness and what I suppose his family thought of as my Protestantism (non-existent as it was) if I continued with our relationship. So, I did what his father wanted, I let Patrick go.

Roz's boyfriend was a local boy, another one who had been away at boarding school and had now come home to work in his father's business. He was generous and good fun, and they would often take me out with them to clubs and pubs. Her relationship with him lasted for a few years. Everyone I knew seemed to be in a couple, which meant I was often alone. I was lonely and lost. I couldn't see a way forward. The intensity of my relationship with Gareth had taken over my life, and although it had been too much at times, there was very little that could live up to that and fulfil my need for passion and excitement.

I wanted to have some money, although I had another two years before I could leave school and earn some. I liked learning, but spending the next few years cramming for exams was not appealing. I wanted to live my life. I felt stifled. The thought crossed my mind that I could run away from all this, but my horizons were so limited that all I could think of was going to London and becoming a prostitute, which I knew I didn't want to do. What I did do was find myself a summer job in Manchester. I went into Manchester on the bus and walked around the shops asking if anyone could give me work. Wiles toyshop on the corner of Market Street and Piccadilly Gardens took me on for six weeks. It was mind-blowingly boring as business was quiet in the summer months. Father drove me in each day as he was on his way to work in the city, and I earned enough money to buy a suede jacket which I'd seen in C & A Modes, and of which I was very proud. It gave me a taste for the rewards of work, which were minimal in Wiles toyshop, but it extended my horizons to that world, where in future I was to find other occupations with much greater rewards.

Part 2

Chapter 19
Tom 1961

I turned fifteen in January 1961. I was plodding on at school, doing the minimum amount of work as I waited for the time when I could leave. My parents and Mr Hardcastle were involved in a court case about the house—Cox versus Hardcastle. It dragged on relentlessly. We'd lived in the house for three years and, by the autumn of 1961, it was in a dire state. The cracks were larger than ever, with a huge one in danger of causing the front bay window to fall completely off the house into the garden. We'd paid to have that side of the house shored up with wooden beams otherwise we wouldn't have been able to live there but there was nothing more we could do about it until the case was settled. You could see right through the four- or five-inch-wide crack to the outside, but Father continued to patch it up with sheets of plywood and plastic. It looked as if the whole front part of the house had been hit by a bomb. We were living in a war zone. The surveyor's report stated that the house had been built on inadequate foundations. It had been built directly on the spot where there had been a pond and a boggy area. Mr Hardcastle appeared not to have taken this into account when he built the foundations. He was to blame, but he employed delaying tactics to avoid facing his responsibilities.

It was the end of the year when the case finally went to court. My father's solicitor argued that the house was worthless as my father clearly couldn't sell it to anyone. My father won the case and Mr Hardcastle was ordered to make good the foundations and the damage to the house, and buy the property back off Father. Mr Hardcastle had to pay the costs of the court case. What soon became clear was that it hadn't been made explicit how much Mr Hardcastle should pay for the house. A letter arrived one day from Mr

Hardcastle's solicitor. Father was sitting at the kitchen table opening his mail. Mother was washing the dishes and I was drying. Father let out a groan and we both turned to look at him. He rested his elbows on the table and put his head in his hands. I knew something awful had happened.

'What is it, Harold?' said Mother.

Father just pushed the letter across the table and Mother sat down and read it. I stood with a plate and a tea towel in my hands and leant against the sink watching them. Father's face was white.

'That's outrageous,' said Mother.

'It's prevarication—pure game-playing,' said Father taking a breath in and sitting upright. 'He knows he must give me at least what I paid for it; I shouldn't be penalised for his negligence.'

Mother turned to me, the letter in her hand. 'It's from Mr Hardcastle's solicitor… he's been ordered to buy the house back off us as part of the settlement—but he's saying that because our solicitor said the house was worthless, he will give us £10 for it—it's an insult.' She turned back to Father with his pale and serious face. 'We'll have to ring the solicitors.'

Negotiations about this insulting offer went back and forth. Like everything to do with this case, it was slow. In the meantime, Mr Hardcastle was supposed to arrange to have concrete pumped under the house to make good the foundations and repair the damage to the house. He didn't move quickly. The people next door had their own claim against Mr Hardcastle ongoing as our house made their house unstable. It was becoming more complicated and lengthier. During this time—it went on for months, then years—Father lost his energy and interest in life. It happened in a way that was hardly perceptible. Seen from the distance of several years, I know it was the beginning of a depression that never left him, and in fact became worse. He had little energy, the pain in his side became worse, and he sat around a great deal with his hand on his right-hand side, nursing the pain and drinking whisky. He managed to work for quite some time in this state, until it overcame him to such an extent that he couldn't continue. The doctor put him on something to relax him, and that made him more tired and slow. He smiled less and less. His face was set in a sad and serious expression most of the time. Mother was tired too. Tired of living in the cold dismal wreck of a house that was our home, tired of being messed with by Mr Hardcastle, tired of Father being tired, probably tired of worrying about me and trying to control me, and tired of being ill herself. The pain in her back had started again and she had to take strong medication to get her through the day. This knocked her out and she rested in the afternoons. I had two worn-out parents collapsing under the weight of the burdens they carried. There was no joy in our house.

One Saturday afternoon I went to Chez with Roz. As we went through the door, I noticed three boys sitting on the scruffy cream leatherette bench in the window. They looked about eighteen. Roz pointed to them, laughed and shouted over.

'Hi, I haven't seen you in here before!' They waved and shouted back.

As we ordered our coffee, Roz told me it was two boys from her school and their friend. We joined them and Roz introduced us: Peter and Mike were in the sixth form at Bury Grammar, and the other one was called Tom. I slid onto the end of the bench nearest to me. I was next to Tom. He showed me his hands, big strong-looking hands, and pointed to his jeans.

'I'm afraid I'm all oily, I've been working on one of our trucks,' he said. 'These two called for me and brought me here before I'd time to go home and change.'

'That's okay,' I said. And it was. 'What was the truck you were mending?' I managed to say although I felt shy in front of these new people. I wished I was more confident like Roz.

'I work for my Father, he's got a business, haulage and

demolition… one of the trucks broke down on Friday afternoon, so I said I'd have a look at it, and try and fix it.'

Tom had a substantial look to him, he was well-built with broad shoulders. His hair was in a sort of James Dean quiff and he was good-looking in a strong-featured sort of way.

'You lot don't usually come in here,' said Roz.

'We heard it's where the prettiest girls come,' said Mike. 'So, we thought we'd take a look.' We all laughed.

'We've been listening to those two arguing and trying to translate what they're saying,' said Peter, looking at Odette and her husband.

'They're always like that,' said Roz, laughing. 'He accuses her of flirting with the customers.' We all laughed again. 'By the way, have you been to the jazz here on a Sunday? It's upstairs—there's not much room, but it's fun.'

'Are you coming here tomorrow?' said Tom, looking at me.

I looked at Roz and we both nodded. 'Yes, let's do that,' she said.

'Can I get you another coffee?' said Tom.

'Oh yes, thanks,' I said.

'How about a piece of apple pie as well?'

'Oh, I don't know…'

'Go on,' he laughed. 'Have a treat on me.'

'Okay, then I will.'

We all had coffee and apple pie, and they offered us a lift home. They were in Peter's mother's car—Mike sat next to Peter, so Roz and I squashed in the back with Tom. I was in the middle as the smallest. I felt the warmth and strength of Tom's thigh pressed next to mine. They dropped us off at Roz's house and we promised to meet them at Chez the following day. I walked home along the railway line. I had liked Tom immediately. His broad shoulders gave him a physique that was substantial looking, and he gave the impression of strength and maturity. He was making his way in life, starting out in something that he was working hard at. There was an air about him that made him seem more of a man than a boy.

On Sunday afternoon, Roz and I made our way to Chez. Tom, Peter and Mike were sitting in the window seat waiting for us. We all went upstairs together. I started to cough almost immediately we entered the room because it was so smoky. The room was very small. Some people were squashed close together sitting on the benches which lined the walls. We five manoeuvred ourselves in. We stood squeezed up against each other so tightly that it was impossible to move. The band, ensconced in one corner, belted out trad jazz. It was so loud I worried that my eardrums might not survive. Their singer, who had a neat little beard, a fancy waistcoat and bowler hat à la Acker Bilk, played the trumpet in between belting out songs. In our restricted spaces we jiggled our heads to the rhythm and swayed our bodies as best we could. The noise of the band—the drums, the bass, the clarinet and, above all, the trumpet—drowned out any attempts at conversation. I was close to Tom. I felt his body next to mine, firm and strong. We exchanged a smile. Roz had ended up a few feet away. She mouthed something to me, but I shook my head, I didn't understand. We were there for about an hour when Tom lifted his hand up as if he was drinking from a cup, mouthing, 'Drink?' I nodded, then signalled and mouthed to Roz that we were going downstairs for a drink. She nodded and gave me a thumbs-up.

'It's quite a relief to get out of there,' I said. 'The smoke and the noise…'

'Yeah,' said Tom. 'Do you want a coffee?'

'Yes please.'

'Will you grab a table while I order?' he said.

I watched him as he ordered coffee. He was wearing a great Scandinavian jumper, dark grey and white with touches of red and blue. It was the latest fashion, and he looked cool. We sat in the window and drank our coffee. I asked him how long he'd been working for his father.

'About a year,' he said. 'I finished my O levels and I was supposed to go back to go into the sixth form. I wasn't sure what I was going to do. I'm interested in flying, so I thought about the Fleet Air Arm, but the life expectancy is only twenty-six, so I thought I might be an architect like my brother, but I didn't want to go back to school to do A levels, so when my father said I could work for him in the holidays, I did, and I stayed.'

'I'm not staying on either, I want to leave as soon as I can,' I said. 'Next summer I'll be gone.'

'What do you want to do?' he said.

'I don't know, probably secretarial—there's not much else if you leave at sixteen,' I said.

'Would you like to go to the pictures some time?' he said.

'I can't go out during the week, but I could go on Friday,' I said.

'I'll give you a ring and I'll pick you up if you like.'

'Okay, that'd be great,'

'Do you fancy a ride out somewhere now?' he said. 'I'd like to go and look at a quarry up on the moors outside Oldham—we're considering buying it. I'm in my mother's Mini. I'll take you home afterwards.'

'Okay, I'll go and tell Roz,' I said.

As we drove out of town, he told me that his father owned a sand quarry nearby. He'd bought it when he came out of the Air Force at the end of the War and he'd sold the sand to the contractors who were building the M62 motorway not far away. Now the quarry was used as a tip. It gave them a base from which to expand the business. Tom said the business had lots of potential, that's why he had stayed. The road climbed up until we were in open moorland. There were no trees, just rocks, heather and tussocks of rough grass. We drew up to roped-off area.

'This is it,' he said. 'Do you want to have a look?'

'Might as well, now we're here.'

We walked to the edge of a high bank where we could look down into the stone quarry.

'What are you thinking of doing with it?' I said.

'Stone extraction—landfill—building maybe,' he said. 'But I'm not sure any of those things would be possible, it's not very big, and it's in the wrong place,' he said. I shivered. He turned to me. 'It's cold, I'll take you home, I just wanted to have a look.'

I put my hand out, palm upwards. 'It's starting to rain.' He grabbed my hand and we ran to the car.

On the way home Tom told me he lived with his mother and his younger sister, and that his parents were divorced. He didn't elaborate and I had a sense that this was an area I shouldn't probe into. We arranged to go to the cinema the following Friday. I was impressed by what he had told me of his father's business. They had ideas to go forward and build it. It made me think he had ambition, which I think may have been, at least partly, his intention, although he turned out not to be any kind of show-off or person impressed by conspicuous wealth. As I came to know him, I saw how focused he was on his job and that that was his driving force. He had found his raison d'être. I hadn't yet found mine.

Tom rang me during the week. His dog at the quarry had had puppies and he wondered if I would like to see them before we went to the cinema on Friday. I said I would, and he came to pick me up. I introduced him to my parents briefly and no one said or did anything embarrassing.

As we drove along, he told me the pups' mother was a guard dog, an Alsatian, and she was possessive of her pups who were only a few days old.

'We can come again if you like when they're a bit older,' he said. 'She might let us cuddle them then.'

'Oh yes, I love animals,' I said. 'I've always wanted a dog, but my parents wouldn't let me have one. I love my cat though.'

The four pups were adorable balls of fluff, all latched onto their mother's teats lying on a blanket in a makeshift cardboard dog bed in a corner of one of the buildings, which clustered at the entrance to the quarry. Their mother growled as we approached, so we stood watching at a distance for a few minutes. I liked that he was fond of animals. I couldn't imagine a life without pets.

'We'd better leave her to it,' said Tom. As we drove away, he pointed to a large, detached house at the front of the quarry.

'That's where we used to live,' he said. 'But my mother couldn't keep it going after the divorce, so it was sold.'

'It looks like a lovely house,' I said.

'It is,' he said.

I stayed quiet; he would tell me more when he was ready. I was at ease with him, and he seemed comfortable and relaxed with me. A pattern for our relationship soon developed. We rarely went out during the week as he was working, and I had school and homework. At weekends, I often spent time with Roz on Saturday afternoons and Sundays, shopping, going to coffee bars, playing tennis. I liked that I still had a life of my own. On Friday and Saturday evenings, Tom and I met the circle of friends we had in pubs or we went to the cinema. Occasionally we went to clubs in Manchester and, as time passed, we would go to a restaurant for a meal, or to a pub that sold bar snacks. We were in the realm of coupledom. Our friends were couples, most of them quite longstanding. Some of them I already knew as friends of the Browns, but some were new to me. I felt grown-up and that I was leading a life that was much better than being at school with its petty restrictions. I loathed having to wear the uniform, it seemed ridiculous to me, all of us, eight hundred girls, every single one of us wearing the same clothes. I tried to customise mine like Cathy had done but always got told off about it. Not the slightest variation was allowed. Shoes, socks, jumpers— everything had to be the same. Even navy-blue knickers had to be worn in the junior school. I sometimes wore make-up but whenever I did, I was sent to wash it off. I did the minimum amount of work to get by. I was lucky that I could do that. Even though I had no plans to continue academic study, I wanted to get a few O levels. Something told me I might be glad of them one day.

After about a month, Tom invited me to meet his mother, Mary, who I of course called Mrs Wright and his younger sister, Julia, who was fourteen and at Bury Grammar School. On the way, we passed the quarry and the house they had lived in before his parents' divorce. It was very unusual to be divorced in the late 1950s, and he told me the story of what had happened gradually over time. Tom's older brother and sister had both been married before the divorce. It was Tom and Julia who'd borne the brunt of the disintegrating marriage. It was a sad and bitter tale of how things had gone so badly wrong that the only way out was divorce. The impact of it on Tom's mother was immense. She now lived in a small, newly built house in Rochdale. She'd only been living there a few months. She'd stayed on in the family home as long as she could with Tom and Julia, supporting herself and them by taking in lodgers. Eventually the family home had been sold, and she had bought the little house they lived in now. Tom's father, Ken, had gone to live with his 'girlfriend' who had left her husband and set up a dress shop. They had her teenage son from her first marriage living with them. In those days with the rarity of divorce, access arrangements for shared parenting seemed to be non-existent. There were certainly no arrangements for Tom and his sister. Tom didn't see his father for two years after the divorce. Financial arrangements also seemed precarious. I never discussed it with Tom's mum, but I assumed she had bought her house from the settlement she received at the time of the divorce. She had a car and received a small 'wage' from Tom's father's business every week but that was all. In the past, she had been a successful dressmaker for years, running a shop and employing several machinists. But broken and depressed by the divorce, she never sewed another garment.

Tom's mother was a plump and pretty woman in her early fifties when I first met her. She was warm and friendly, touching me as she spoke. I was unused to this; my own mother was not at all affectionate and my instinct was to recoil from Mary's touch. I managed not to do that, and gradually I grew to accept it and enjoy her warmth.

'I've heard a lot about you,' she said, as Tom, standing next to her, rolled his eyes. 'All good I might add.' She also called me Carol a few times. Tom rolled his eyes again. Carol had been Tom's previous girlfriend, but it only made me laugh.

Julia arrived home with a Victoria sponge cake for tea, and we had ham salad with bread and butter, and the cake afterwards. Julia was also plump like her mum, and even more shy than I was, prone to blushing easily. Mary talked about her two older children and her grandchildren. Tom said he thought we might visit his older sister, Barbara, and her husband, Dan, and their two small children soon.

Two weeks later, we set off in Mary's Mini to meet Dan and Babs, as Tom called her. They lived in a caravan on a residential site in Southport. Tom told me about them as we drove there. They'd been married for five years and had two children aged four and two, a boy and a girl. Dan was an architect and had been at Heywood Grammar School and Manchester Art School with Stuart, Tom's older brother. I thought living in a caravan was romantic, and I was excited about meeting them and seeing their place. The site was set back off the main road and the caravans were well spaced out, with little gardens around them. Bushes and trees screened the site from the road. Tom drove along the narrow track, turning off to park next to a caravan that stood further back than those on either side, within a circle of mature trees and bushes. I liked this idea of a family with children living in a caravan. It was like being in a Noel Streatfeild book or permanently on holiday. Tom had told me that Stuart and his wife, Patsy, also had two children of similar ages to Dan and Barbara's. I started to feel nervous as we drew up. A young woman opened the caravan door and stepped out. I recognised immediately her likeness to her mother, although Barbara was taller and slimmer than Mary.

'Hello,' she smiled. 'You must be Beth.'

'Yes,' I smiled back. 'Hello.'

'Come on in, it's chilly out here—we don't have a lot of space, but we'll fit you in.'

Inside the caravan was neat and modern, with clean lines, and as I took it all in, I saw doors and flaps and drawers everywhere—overhead and underneath seating— all the space was utilised. A tiny kitchen area equipped with a cooker, a fridge and a sink led to a main living room with an open fire. Two armchairs, a bench and a fold-up table still left room for their two small children to run trains around a track on the floor. I thought it was lovely and said so.

'Well, it's fine for now,' said Babs. 'There are two bedrooms through there, we manage pretty well.'

Dan was a stocky, good-looking man with bright blue eyes. He smiled and gestured to us to take a seat on the bench. The children, whom I thought were extraordinarily beautiful, had stopped what they were doing and stared at us with big eyes.

'Peter and Marianne,' said Barbara.

'Hello,' I said. They both stared at me.

'Take a seat, Beth,' said Babs. 'I'll put the kettle on.'

I felt at home. I liked what I saw. It was a tiny space but there was enough room for two adults and two children; it was a place to share with people you loved.

Chapter 20

Secrets and Lies 1962

It was the end of February 1962, a Sunday, and it was the day when I should have started my period except that I didn't. I was regular, my cycle was short, three weeks and three or four days. I might occasionally be early, but I was never late. I knew on that day that I was pregnant.

For most of the time, I sat in the lounge reading, pretending I was doing my homework, but I was thinking about my situation. Two bars on the electric fire gave out intense heat for about a yard in front but nothing to the rest of the room. The room was dingy and depressing due to the crumbling wall and bay window, which had been shored up with great planks of wood outside. The roughly patched-up cracks, the partially removed red wallpaper Mother had chosen for the alcoves, and the shabby gold striped wallpaper on the other walls all added to the miserable atmosphere. But I could ignore all that as I had more urgent things to think about. The idea that I was pregnant was taking shape in my mind. I had a strong urge to keep it from Mother. I needed time to think about what I wanted to do. And so, I began a life of lies.

The first thing I had to lie about was my non-existent period. I had to feign that I had the usual period pains and that I was having a quiet day because of that. Over the past year the pains had grown less, and I was no longer sick, but I usually had to ask Mother for some paracetamol, and to buy me some sanitary towels, so I had to start lying straight away. I worked out I was probably about two or three weeks' pregnant. In four months' time, in June, I was due to take my O Level examinations and then I would leave school. I was enrolled at a secretarial college in Manchester to do a year's course, but my heart was certainly not in it. I had vaguely thought I might find a job somewhere interesting like Granada Studios.

Tom and I had started taking risks after my sixteenth birthday in January. We were both young and healthy, and we both knew what was going to happen. Why did we do that? This was a question I have asked myself many times throughout my life. I was desperate to change my life and impatient to grow up and have control. I loathed school and living in our crumbling house in equal measure. I wanted some fun, some joy. Mother was not well and was low in spirits caused by her health, and the ongoing problem with the house. This impacted on Father, who had his own health concerns. The pain in his side had been investigated and showed nothing physical. We had known it all along. It was his nerves and he was unlikely to improve until all the problems they both had were resolved. And that was not likely to happen quickly or even at all. Taking the risks Tom and I took was going to lead to one obvious outcome. We had gone into it with our eyes open.

'I could get pregnant,' I'd said.

'I'll look after you, I promise,' he'd said.

Did I want that? Did I want a baby? Did I want to be with him? Yes, I did. I did want a family; I'd always wanted a family. If he changed his mind about it, I'd be alone. Except I thought my parents would also support me if necessary. I knew they wouldn't throw me out or anything drastic like that. But that wasn't what I wanted. I wanted a new life with a family of my own. But I suspected that that wouldn't be what Mother wanted. She had ambitions for me. I was about to let down both her and Father. I could hardly bear to think about these consequences and what I would have to go through with my parents. They would be hurt, and they had enough worries without this. There were other options of course. Abortion was illegal, but there were ways round this. It was possible to find a doctor who would be willing to use their discretion and agree to perform one if you could pay and if you said you couldn't cope with a baby. That might be Mother's preference. Or, you might find someone who did the job illegally, a back-street abortionist, but this idea terrified me. I might be damaged or even die as a result of that. I began to realise that what I had inside me, a baby, was precious, it would be mine and I wanted to keep it. I couldn't envisage getting rid of it. There was another alternative, which I thought Mother might prefer. Because of the terrible shame and stigma attached to having a baby before you were married which still prevailed in 1962, and because a safe termination was not easy to come by, many unmarried girls had their babies in special mother and baby homes, and gave their babies up for adoption. But that seemed the worst of all possible options. What I wanted was for Tom and me to make a home together, and to bring up a family. I thought that was what he wanted, but I wasn't certain, nor was I sure whether Mother and Father would want this either. I would wait to talk to Tom as soon as I saw him next weekend. After all, I might start my period the next day.

I didn't start my period the next day or the one after, or the one after that. I knew in the deepest core of my being that I was pregnant. I told Tom and he was relaxed about it, saying that whatever I wanted to do, he would support me. But he thought we should try and get something to make me start my period. He would ask around. I agreed to that, but I was reluctant to try anything that I didn't know for sure what it was I was taking. And when two weeks later he presented me with what looked like a cough medicine bottle full of brown-coloured liquid, I was full of foreboding. There were no labels on it, and it smelled faintly of liquorice.

'Two teaspoons morning and night,' he said. He looked me. 'But don't take it if you don't want to.'

I took the bottle and hid it in my underwear drawer. There it lay until I threw it away a few weeks later. I told Tom I didn't want to get rid of the baby and that I didn't want to tell anyone, most of all my mother, until after I had finished my O levels in June. The reason for this was that I was sure that at that stage she would put pressure on me to have an abortion. And I wanted to be sure and clear about what I wanted, and what we, Tom and I, together wanted. I also wanted to take my O levels without the added pressure that would occur if my parents knew about the baby. Tom said we'd work it out together, he had been thinking we'd get married in a year or two anyway, when I'd got a job and we'd saved up some money. It was just bringing everything forward a year or two. He thought his mother would be supportive, he said. She liked me. We could always tell Babs and Dan at some point—he knew they would also be understanding and helpful. He thought his brother Stuart and his wife, Patsy, would also be understanding, and he wanted me to meet them and their two young children. They lived near his mother in Rochdale. Stewart was an architect employed by the council and, by virtue of that, had managed to procure a council house for them. Both these architect brothers-in-law had plans to design and build their own houses in the future. I said I wanted to tell Janet, who I could trust, and probably Roz at some point, but Janet first. And what about his father?

'Leave him out of it for the moment,' he said. 'It's none of his business.'

And so we carried on like this, no one knowing, except Janet, who wasn't surprised. She was the best friend ever, keeping the secret, and helping me when I fainted twice in what we called 'prayers', when the whole school met together in the large hall. We had bible readings and hymns and we knelt to pray, which was when I fainted. Because of my history with troubled periods, the games teacher who took me to the sick bay assumed that was the reason. I carried my secret close; the knowledge of it gave me a purpose in life. I had decided I would have this baby and look after it. The baby filled the gap in my life, completed me, matured me, gave me a purpose, and I was happier than I had been for a long time, I knew where I was going. I loved my parents and I knew they loved me. They did their best for me, but I always had the feeling they didn't know what to do with me. I was too much in some way, wanting and needing too much. The life I had was not the life I wanted. My parents, battered and bashed about by illness, and worries over money and the house problem, could only just keep on going. Tom was in a similar situation, parents who had too many of their own problems to have much energy left for anything else. We both wanted to get away from our present lives and start a new life together. This was never articulated in so many words, rather it was a communication on a deeper level that drew us together and kept us together. Tom and I were each, in similar but also in individual ways, slightly off kilter and unconventional. We recognised that in each other. So, I went about school and homework calmer than I'd ever been. We would have to face up to our families soon, but not quite yet.

As I look back, I am amazed at how limited my horizons were and how impatient and desperate I was for something that would give meaning to my life. I could have concentrated on my studies; in a couple of years I could have been at university, but this held no appeal at all. I'd not met many people who were at or who had been to university. I did meet a young woman when Mother and I were visiting my mother's sister-in-law, Aunt Barbara who had married my mother's youngest brother. Aunt Barbara was quite posh and lived in Bristol. This young woman talked a lot, was very confident and swore a lot, which was unusual. I didn't feel I would fit in if this was what people were like at university. That was a very naive response, of course, and I think I was just confirming to myself that it would not be for me. I think I was scared and allowed this experience to show me what I wanted to see. It felt like not much was open to me. And no one had the time, energy or interest in talking to me. I needed an anchor and a baby would provide it.

Chapter 21
Pregnancy 1962

As the weeks went by, I had to try and hide morning sickness from my mother. On one occasion I vomited near the tennis club on my way to the bus, having managed to control it at home. Fortunately, I didn't suffer too much from it, but she heard me vomiting in the toilet one morning and asked me later if there was anything I wanted to tell her. I was tempted to say something, but I didn't, then as the weeks went by and I began to put on weight, she asked me again. It was May. The O level examinations were due to start at the beginning of June. During that time, we were only required to go into school for the exams we were sitting. The rest of the time was free. It meant I didn't have the dreaded early mornings every day and the sickness that went with that, and the constant worry of someone guessing I was pregnant, although I hardly showed at all and no one had any idea. But now my mother was asking more questions. I talked to Tom and we agreed that maybe the time had come to tell her. But before we put any plans forward, I wanted to know what he wanted to do, what he really wanted to do, not what he thought he should do. I asked him to think about it. I told him I knew my parents would help me if he didn't want to, and that I didn't want him to feel an obligation to be with me, or to do anything he didn't want to do. I said he could take as long as he wanted to decide, and that we should have no contact during that time.

Tom and I had become used to regular phone calls—almost every evening. Our telephone was in the hall, which was the coldest place in the house, and there was no privacy as people were always on their way up or down stairs or from room to room. Despite these deterrents, we often spoke at length, so I thought Mother or Father would have noticed that Tom hadn't been phoning recently. But they didn't. What with the house problem still lingering on in the legal ether and being preoccupied with their own health problems, they didn't have much time and energy for anything else. I felt so guilty about the fact that I knew my mother was worrying about me. It was unbearable to think about it. But what happened next to cause them yet more worry about the house saga was that Mr Hardcastle employed the ultimate delaying tactic—he died—and Mrs Hardcastle, in a futile attempt to avoid what she had to do, which was to buy my parents' house back off them for a reasonable amount of money, reacted by not claiming probate, holding the whole thing up further. And that was what they talked about at mealtimes—that and what they would do when this was all over.

The plan was to buy a bungalow in Kent, where my father had been stationed during the War when he was in the Army. Although travelling had been difficult during the War, Mother had managed to go on the train to see Father a few times. They had harboured a fantasy of living there ever since and now they thought that the time was coming when it could become a reality. Father was even looking for a job in Kent, and thinking and planning for this bright new future cheered them up.

After a week, Tom phoned me and asked if we could meet. He came to collect me on Friday evening, and we went to our favourite pub. He told me that he wanted to be with me and that he would like us to marry. I said that was what I wanted too. We discussed the possibility that my symptoms could be due to something else and that we should be sure beyond any doubt that I was pregnant before we told our families. In those days, before home pregnancy tests, I would have to see a doctor. I didn't want to go to our family doctor, so we chose one nearby whose consulting rooms we regularly drove past. The next day, Tom collected me from home in the morning. We told my parents we were going to see his grandfather then drove straight into the small car-parking area outside the doctor's surgery. Two different doctors' names were on a plaque next to the door and a list of surgery times showed they had a Saturday-morning surgery. I went in, leaving Tom in the car, and asked the receptionist if I could see a doctor. It seemed to be no problem that I wasn't registered as a patient and, after a short wait, I was shown in to see the doctor. He was probably in his fifties, he looked old to me, but he also looked kind. I had immediate confidence that he would try to help me. He listened to my story attentively and said he would like his wife, who was also a doctor, to examine me. She must have retained her maiden name to avoid confusion. She was summoned and she was kind like her husband. There was no judgement or shock in her manner and voice, and she looked homely.

I had to lie on the couch, and she gave me an internal examination, the first I'd ever had. As I lay there on my back, legs akimbo and the doctor poking about inside me, I realised I would probably be having more of these inelegant examinations in the future. And yes, I was pregnant. We sat and talked. She asked me what I wanted to do, and she encouraged me to tell my parents as soon as I could. I thanked her. Both doctors had given me a good experience, which was not always to be the case when my pregnancy, my age and my marital status, or lack of it, was revealed.

Tom and I had been going regularly to see Babs and Dan at weekends, and Tom thought we should share the secret with them first, so they could support Tom's mother through it all. Tom was worried about how his mother would cope with this. The divorce had been such a trauma for her; she hadn't been the same since. Tom hadn't mentioned his father again. I thought it best to leave that subject for the time being.

We went to Southport for the day. It was May but it was cold, and Dan and Babs had a fire going in the caravan. The children, dressed up warmly in jackets and hats, were playing in a little sandpit in the garden. After a few preliminary exchanges of how everyone was, Dan went out to fill the coal scuttle and check on the children, and Tom just blurted it out.

'Babs,' he said. 'Beth's pregnant.'

Babs's mouth fell open and she stared at us for what seemed like a long time, but it was only the time it took for Dan to fill the scuttle and come back in. Dan put some coal on the fire, replaced the fireguard and sat down. He looked around at us.

'What?' he said.

'There's going to be another baby in the family,' said Babs, now smiling. Dan looked at her, trying to make sense of what she'd said.

'It's us,' said Tom. 'Beth's pregnant.'

'Well,' said Dan. 'It's only natural isn't it?'

There followed an intense conversation about all the details of when the baby was due, and what our plans were. So far, we'd formulated that we wanted to get married. We wanted to be together and make a family of our own. We planned to tell my parents the following week and then Tom's mother after that.

'Oh, it's going to be hard to keep quiet, Mum and Julia are coming over next Sunday,' said Babs. 'But don't worry, I won't say anything. What about Dad?' She turned to Tom.

'I'll tell him when I'm ready,' said Tom. He set his face in a firm look that said 'leave it'.

Tom and I decided to tell my parents on the following Friday evening. We were in the front room watching television with Mother, when Father, who was working the following day, went up to bed. I looked at Tom, it's now, we must do this. He put the back of his hand up to his nose and held it there. There was a spot of blood on his hand. He pulled a handkerchief out of his pocket and put it to his nose. Bright red blood began to soak the hanky. He looked at me.

'My nose is bleeding,' he said. 'It's okay, it's not much.' I looked at Mother.

'We've got something to tell you,' I said. She got up and turned off the television. She sat down and looked at us both.

'I know,' she said. 'I've been waiting.' She looked old, sad and tired. 'What are you going to do about it?'

'We want to get married,' I said.

'We'll see about that,' she said and got up again. 'I'm going to tell your father.'

Mother went upstairs. I turned to Tom and started to cry. I hated to hurt Mother like this. He put his arm round me and dabbed at his nose with his other hand. We sat and waited. After a few minutes, Mother came downstairs followed by Father. Mother was crying, and Father looked very serious. He wasn't angry, he seemed more hurt and vulnerable. I felt so bad. They both sat down and looked at us.

'Your mother has told me...' said Father. 'What are we going to do?' His voice quivered. I thought he was going to cry.

'We want to get married,' I said.

'Is that what you want, Tom?' said Father.

'Yes, that's what I want,' said Tom.

'You don't have to,' said Mother. 'There are other ways round this.'

'We want to get married,' I said.

'But you've no money and nowhere to live,' Mother said. 'Besides, your education... if you gave the baby away, you could carry on with your education, not waste it.'

'We'll find somewhere to live,' said Tom. 'I'm working.'

'What about your parents?' said Father. 'Do they know?'

'Not yet,' said Tom. 'We'll tell my mum at the weekend and my dad... my parents are divorced...'

'Why have you left it so late to tell me,' said Mother, who was crying again. 'Why didn't you tell me before?'

'Because I knew you'd want me to get rid of it or give it

away.' I started crying again.

'You could still do that,' said Mother. 'What about your O levels?'

'I'm going to take them.'

There was silence apart from Mother and me sitting opposite each other crying. Neither of us could move to comfort the other.

'I think we should leave it for now and sleep on it,' said Father. 'I need to take it in.'

Silently we all agreed. We knew that was the best thing to do. There was no point going over it again. We'd stated our positions, and we all needed some time and space to think about it. Tom stood up, glad to escape. I went to the front door with him and we kissed goodbye. I went up to bed and I heard my parents talking downstairs. They soon followed me upstairs. I was in bed crying. Mother came in. She sat on the bed and stroked my face.

'Don't worry,' she said gently. 'We'll sort it out together, it'll be all right.'

'I feel so bad,' I said.

'We'll look after you as best we can,' she said. 'Try and get some sleep.' I cried myself to sleep that night.

Tom told his mother and she was lovely about it. She said we mustn't give the child away, that she would look after it, if that's what it came to. She said she'd hoped that Tom and I would stay together and eventually get married, so what did it matter if it was only a year or two earlier than planned. I was eternally grateful to her for that. It was arranged that she would drive over to meet my parents. She came the following weekend, wearing her best hat, and her suit with the fur collar that she'd worn at Babs and Dan's wedding. And she came with a plan. Babs and Dan had been looking at new houses, and they'd put a deposit down on one in Ormskirk. They said we could live with them until we had a home of our own, as there was plenty of room for all of us. After more discussion between the parents, this was the solution that everyone thought was for the best. It didn't take long for Mother to come around to my way of thinking about not giving away, or in any way getting rid of the baby.

It was all planned. First, I had to sit my O levels in June. I was still able to fit into my school uniform, and I managed to get through the next couple of weeks until it was time for the exams. I did as much revision as I could, although not much stayed in my head. I had too many other things on my mind. The exams went on for two weeks. After that it was the annual Wakes Weeks—Bolton holidays—a hangover from the days when the cotton industry ruled the town, and everything closed for a fortnight and the workers went to Blackpool for day trips, or longer if they could afford it. We were then expected to go back to school for another two weeks to complete the term. I didn't do this. My time at Bolton School finished the day I sat my last O level.

It was after my exams that I finally met Tom's father. He came around to meet me and my parents one weekend in June. Tom had taken his time telling him we were getting married, saying that Ken hadn't told him when he got married the previous year to Jean, the woman he'd been having an affair with for the past eleven years. Ken was quite a character, good-looking and always well dressed, but a bit of a rough diamond. He'd worked part-time in a cotton mill from the age of twelve, which was what happened to children from working-class families when he was a boy. He'd married Mary when they were both in their early twenties, like my parents, and Stuart and Barbara were born in the years before the outbreak of the Second World War. During the War, Ken was called up, like my father, and, from what I've learned about him since, he seemed to spend most of his time in the Royal Air Force painting pin-up girls on aircraft for the pilots. He liked pubs, drinking, smoking, gambling and women. He was also a wheeler-dealer, and after the War sold army surplus goods, and the vegetables he'd grown, on the markets. There were many stories about him. One was that he bought up army surplus gravy boats which he sprayed with different-coloured paints, planted up with bulbs, and sold on the markets. He was famous for his market call: 'Roll up, roll up, two for the price of one.' Some of his ventures were successful and some were not. We probably didn't know about the less successful ones. He'd bought the sand quarry, where his current business was based, after the War. That was one of his better moves, and he'd struck lucky through selling sand and then using the site as a tip. A steady stream of lorries rolled into the quarry and tipped waste there.

The plans for our future were taking shape. Everyone who needed to know was told. The wedding date was set, and it was agreed that we would live in Ormskirk with Dan and Babs until we had a place of our own. It was an immense relief to leave school. Tom continued to live with his mother and Julia, and I continued to live with my parents until we married. I was happy.

Chapter 22

Marriage 1962

Tom and I were married on 8th August 1962 at Holcombe Parish Church. The vicar was the father of two of the girls who had travelled on the bus to school with me every day. I wondered what he thought about it. He avoided eye contact with me throughout the marriage service. He did his job in a detached way. We had needed parental permission and the permission of a church dignitary as we were under twenty-one. Tom was nineteen and I was sixteen. It was a very small wedding with no official photographer and no fancy white dress, although we did go to a pub where they served good food for a meal afterwards, and my mother took a few photographs. Tom and I didn't care that we didn't have a fancy wedding, or that we didn't have our own home—we just wanted to get it over and done with. Roz was my bridesmaid, and Tom's friend Hugh was the best man. Roz's mother had made her a new skirt and jacket, and Hugh wore his only suit. I had a new skirt with a loose jacket and Tom had a new suit. Roz and I wore hats. John, my brother, came to the wedding. He asked, not in a judgemental way, why I had done this—he thought, correctly, that I probably couldn't wait to get away. He was planning to go back to London as soon as he could, saying he couldn't bear to stay in our dismal house with our ill and depressed parents.

After a few days' honeymoon in the Lake District—where we stayed in the Sun Inn at Pooley Bridge, which was noted for its food at the time, and where we did some walking and exploring, and Tom swam in the freezing waters of Ullswater—we set up home with Babs and Dan in Ormskirk in their new, modern, spacious house. We slept in a downstairs bedroom in a bed that was a wedding gift from my parents, and in our new wedding present sheets from Aunty Elsie and Uncle George. Tom's father had bought him a new minivan, and, as Ormskirk was too far for Tom to reasonably travel to work every day, he regularly stayed over at his mother's during the week. I helped Babs with the housework and cooking, and looked after the children while she took driving lessons. That was how we lived for the next three months. Not long after we arrived in Ormskirk in August, I went to a telephone box to ring up school and find out my O Level results. Not surprisingly I had only passed three: English Language, English Literature and French. I was disappointed. I'd thought I might have managed Needlework and History. But it made me realise how my pregnancy had affected my mind. It had entirely displaced everything else. Fortunately, that was a temporary state and I was to discover in the future that I had a brain that I could use.

Our baby was due in November. I had to register with a doctor and at the local maternity unit. Mother and Father usually came over to visit me in Ormskirk on a Wednesday as it was Father's day off. They took me to the hospital on one of these occasions and I was registered as a patient by a po-faced receptionist, who looked me up and down when my age was revealed, and who was automatically putting down my parents as next-of-kin until I told her I was married. I saw the doctor and then a midwife. I was weighed, examined and had all the checks I should have had done much earlier in my pregnancy, but everything was fine, and I left with another appointment to come back in a month's time. The baby's due date was 5th November. Bonfire Night.

I enjoyed staying with Babs and Dan. Most of my time was spent with Babs and the children. Babs had been a dressmaker like her mother before she married, and she helped me to improve my sewing skills. She showed me how to use her state-of-the-art sewing machine to make little nightdresses for the baby. Boy and girl babies wore nightdresses for the first few weeks of their lives in 1962.

There were no Babygrows and no disposable nappies in those days. I had to start preparing a layette, buying terry-towelling nappies off the market and knitting little jackets. I learned more about cooking and baking off Babs, and I helped her with the clothes washing and childcare. Tom came over on Friday nights and stayed until Monday morning.

As the time passed, I went more often to the ante-natal clinic and, during the last three weeks of my pregnancy as 5th November approached, I went every week. Bonfire Night came and went. Dan set off a little firework display for the children, and I sat and watched it with them. I went to the clinic on 7th November. Everything was fine. They sent me home to wait. At the 14th November clinic, they told me that it was preferable that I went into labour naturally, but if nothing had happened by the 21st November clinic, I was to bring my bag with me, and they would admit me and induce labour. Tom had stayed with his mother for the weekend as he had to mend her car and do some work on a lorry, and on the evening of Saturday 17th November, I began to have contractions. I also had a show of blood and Babs thought it was time to take me in. It was 11pm. Babs drove me to the hospital and went in with me. At that time, it was unusual even for husbands to stay with a woman in labour, so no one mentioned to Babs that she might stay. I had no expectation that she would either, but I felt lonely saying goodbye to her. I wished Tom was there.

I had to have an enema, a bath and a pubic shave. The enema was uncomfortable, and I was shown the toilet and the bathroom, and left to get on with it. The contractions became stronger after the enema and, as soon as I got in the bath, I needed the toilet again. I dried myself and put my nightdress and dressing gown on. I was bent double by a contraction halfway down the corridor to the toilet, but I struggled on. After I'd finished, I rang the buzzer I'd been shown, and a midwife appeared and took me into the labour

175

room. She examined me and said it would probably be some time before the baby came, but to ring if I needed anything. I was alone in a clinical-looking room with oxygen cylinders, a row of cupboards and a sink in one corner. I was lying on a high couch. There was a clock on the wall, and I watched the hours ticking by as my contractions became ever stronger. I was in increasing pain. I felt so alone and didn't know when I could reasonably ask for help. I didn't want to be a nuisance and bring down the wrath of these nurses on me. I was embarrassed by my situation and knew I was a target for anyone who had prejudices about pregnant sixteen-year-olds. It was the sensation of needing to go to the toilet that decided me. I knew I would not make it off the couch and to the toilet as the pain was so severe. I rang the buzzer and the midwife came. She examined me.

'You don't need the toilet,' she said. 'It's the baby coming.'

Thank goodness I rang for help at the right time. Another midwife appeared. She gave me an injection for the pain and instructed me to lie on my back with my legs akimbo. Another crippling pain spread from my abdomen around my back and I moaned.

'Do you feel like you want to push?'

'Yes,' I gasped.

'Push,' she said. 'Push.' I felt the baby straining to come out, but I thought I might split wide open if I pushed so at the next contraction I pushed and resisted the urge to push at the same time.

'Push into your bottom, not your throat,' said one of the nurses. 'One more push, come on, you can do it, push this baby out.' My legs were wide apart and supported on the shoulders of each midwife. I gave one almighty painful push and my baby emerged into the world. Alicia Jane was born at 4.25am on 18th November 1962. After more contractions the afterbirth appeared.

'A healthy little girl, weighing six pounds four ounces—you've done well,' they said. 'No stitches and a quick labour.'

That was the only praise I was ever to receive in that place. They showed Alicia to me then took her away. What did she look like? I wanted to see her properly. All I glimpsed was a crinkled little face. She had to be washed, they said. I was washed and given a pill and told to sleep. I didn't think I needed a pill, but I took it anyway. I had just done the hardest work I had ever done in the whole of my short life and I had missed a night's sleep. I was very tired, and I slept immediately and deeply. I woke up as I was being bundled into a wheelchair by a nurse and porter.

'Wake up, love, you're going to the ward now.'

They covered me with a blanket and took me along miles of corridors to a large ward full of other mothers and babies. They wheeled me to an empty bed about halfway down the ward, lifted me onto it and left. I looked around. There must have been about twenty women in the ward, which was of the old-fashioned Nightingale type. We could all see each other. I watched as the other mothers began to take their babies out of the little cots that were at the end of their beds. Some of the mothers looked quite old, others were in their twenties. There was another very young mother, but she seemed much more confident than me and chatted to the other women in a loud voice. One or two nurses came in carrying babies, which they gave to their mothers. It was feeding time, and some of the women were being helped to feed and change their babies, while others were getting on with it by themselves. There was no baby at the end of my bed, so I plucked up courage and asked a passing nurse where mine was.

'In the nursery,' she said, edging away as she spoke.

'Is she all right?' I was scared and worried. Where was my baby?

'Yes, we'll bring her in later.' And that was it. No one seemed very concerned about me or my baby, so I tried not to worry too much. I sat in my bed feeling lonely and sad. One of the older women came over to me after she'd fed her baby and put it back in its cot.

'Are you all right, love?' she said.

'They haven't brought my baby out of the nursery...' I said fighting back tears.

'When did you have it?' she said.

'She was born last night—I mean this morning, at twenty-five past four.'

'It's early days yet,' she said. 'They'll bring her out soon enough, try not to worry.'

I laid back against the pillows and dozed off. It was the clatter of dishes and cutlery that woke me up. It was lunchtime. They brought me a tray and I picked at the food, a not very appetising cottage pie and peas followed by semolina pudding. It was marginally better than school dinners. After lunch, two nurses came around the ward with a trolley. They went to every patient and drew the curtains round each bed. They came to wash us, change our sanitary pads and inspect us. I felt clean and fresh afterwards, and while they were doing it, I asked about Alicia.

'We'll bring her to you as soon as we've finished the round,' they said. 'Get up and put one of your maternity bras on and you can start breastfeeding her.'

From the beside locker, they passed me one of the huge maternity bras I had brought in with me. I lifted up my nightie and fitted the bra on over my now massive breasts. They'd been steadily increasing in size throughout my pregnancy, but now they were even bigger, with a network of blue veins criss-crossed all over them and my previously pink nipples now brown. I hadn't expected they would be so huge. I felt a surge of excitement and joy when they brought Alicia to me wrapped in a hospital blanket and laid her on the bed. They showed me how to change her nappy. It was the first time I'd seen her properly. She was tiny, although not a bad birth weight. Her fingers and toes gripped mine as I examined her tiny nails. I marvelled at her delicate eyebrows and eyelashes, and I thought she had her father's strong nose. I inspected her whole body; she was perfect and beautiful. Intense, powerful love stirred in my heart and quickened my pulse. My baby girl, she needed me. I would look after her and do my best for her.

'Now we'll help you to feed her,' said one of the nurses. 'Sit down, undo your bra at the front and hold her in your arms so her head and mouth are just under your breast. Hold her head firmly.'

I was not at all prepared for what followed. Alicia was sleepy, and me and my breasts (they didn't feel as if they belonged to me), unused as we were to feeding a baby, could not get the hang of it. The nurses gently pulled at my smooth full nipples to give Alicia the mouthful of nipple that she needed to be able to latch onto. Despite my pulling out my nipples as instructed during pregnancy they didn't protrude enough for a baby to latch onto. Especially a sleepy baby like Alicia. She slid off and went to sleep. They showed me again how to try and pull my nipple out and put one in Alicia's mouth, and left me to it. It was a frustrating half hour. I felt increasingly useless and finally gave up. My not managing to breastfeed, surely a natural and easy enough process, felt like a failure. The nurses said not to worry, Alicia would soon be more alert, and they'd give her a drink of water in the nursery. They brought her to me again at 6 pm, and the process was repeated. They took her back to the nursery again where they would keep an eye on her, they said. I wanted to keep her with me as I expected Tom would be visiting that evening. But no, he could look at her in the nursery if he wanted to, they said.

I scanned the faces of the men who came through the double doors of the ward, hoping to see Tom's. I smiled to myself as I recognised the father of the baby whose mother was the other very young mum on the ward. The baby looked exactly like its father. The flow of visitors stilled as they all found their wives and babies. Tom was nearly half an hour late. He'd driven from Bury after working all day on a lorry and had had to get washed and changed. He said he'd look at Alicia on his way out as there wasn't much visiting time left. I told him she was sleepy, and he said that was a family trait. He was pleased to see me and happy that the birth had gone well, and that we were both healthy and Alicia was perfect. He said he would have liked a boy, but he would love Alicia and maybe we would have some more children. I said I was sure she and I would get the hang of feeding soon enough. He told me that my parents were coming on Wednesday to see us and he hoped we'd be home soon. In the meantime, he wouldn't come again, he was going back to Bury early in the morning, as work was busy the next day. It was tiring for him to keep driving over and it was dark so early in the evening now, and again early in the morning. I understood, but I wished I could see more of him. I longed to be with him and to be home. He kissed me goodbye and left just before visiting time was over so he could see Alicia.

The next day was another day of frustrating lack of feeding progress. I was starting to feel desperately worried about Alicia. Wouldn't she be needing milk? Couldn't we try and give her bottle? This request was met with pursed lips and a shake of the head. No, we would stay in hospital until Alicia was settled at the breast and that was that. On the third day, my parents came to visit in the afternoon. They explained to a nurse that it was my father's day off and that they'd come a long way, and would the staff be kind enough to let them in to see their daughter and granddaughter. A nurse let them in, and they smiled and exclaimed over Alicia, who was sleeping in the cot at the end of my bed. They wanted to know how I was and what it was like there. I was explaining the feeding problems when the Sister appeared on the ward. She said that the other, junior, nurse shouldn't have let visitors in; it wasn't visiting time and they would have to leave. My father explained the situation again, but she wouldn't budge. My father said he would like to see her superior to complain about this lack of understanding and they all left, my parents turning to wave at the ward doors. They didn't return. Babs came that evening. We talked about my feeding problems. She said she'd not breastfed her two babies, and she didn't know why they were so rigid about it. I was feeling desperate by this time and Babs said she'd ring Tom and tell him what was going on. Perhaps if things didn't improve, he could take me out of there, and back to her house, and we'd put Alicia on a bottle.

The next day was the worst day of all. My already monstrous breasts had become even more engorged and hard. It was even less likely now that Alicia would latch on properly and suck. She'd lost weight; this was usual, but she was so small that I was worrying about her survival. I started to cry when another feeding struggle ended in failure. Alicia was perking up now, she was hungry, so she was frustrated too and crying loudly. Yet again we were sitting there after all the other mothers had fed their babies and settled them down. A nurse came over to me. I was sitting there holding Alicia in my arms with tears streaming down my face, crying silently.

'How old are you?' said the nurse as she tried to help me.
'Sixteen.'

'You're very young.' Her tone was disapproving.

'I'm worried about my baby, if she doesn't feed soon, she'll die.' More tears and sobs.

'No, she won't,' she said. 'We won't let that happen, your milk's come in properly today and it's engorged your breasts, you've got plenty of milk, so that's a good thing and once she starts sucking the engorgement will ease off.'

'How can you stop it from happening when you won't give her a bottle. I've tried and I can't do it, I can't breastfeed, please let me give her a bottle.' I was sobbing now.

'Look, don't get upset, I'll see what I can do,' she said more kindly. 'I'll look after her in the nursery, we're going to take her back in there anyway because she's not feeding, and I'll tell you when I've given her a bottle and we'll see how she goes. But don't tell anyone, we're not supposed to do it. In the meantime, you might try massaging your breasts so the milk will start to flow; they won't allow breast pumps, you have to do it by hand.'

This nurse was one of the kinder ones. There were two who I'd worked out were the kindest, and most likely to help from their manner when they came to examine me and help me with feeding. This one was Irish with black hair that curled round her pretty face. Her blue eyes were fringed with dark lashes, and she was calm and quiet. The other kind one was just the opposite. She had massive breasts herself, which were out of all proportion with the rest of her tiny body. She had a plain face with straight mousey hair, and she was noisy and talkative. But she listened and didn't fob me off, and she did what she said she would do. These were the two that I looked for when I needed help with anything. Some of the other mothers were kind too. They came to ask how I was and complained about their stitches and their piles and marvelled at my lack of any such things. They admired my flat stomach, which had almost gone back to its pre-pregnancy state. Some of them looked as if they were still pregnant. They were kind and tried to reassure me about my feeding problems.

The following day the Matron came to do a ward round. She paraded around all the beds with the Sister. They stopped in front of my bed. She looked at Alicia in her cot.

'Is this the baby whose grandfather thinks we have nothing better to do with our time than accommodate people who come to visit outside of visiting hours?' she said in a loud voice.

'Yes, Matron,' said the Sister.

'And whose young mother is having problems breastfeeding her child?'

'Yes, Matron.'

She fixed her eyes on me. 'We'll keep you here until your baby is settled at the breast, however long that takes.'

I was deeply hurt and angry and very anxious about my baby girl. What gave her the right to treat me like that? I couldn't take much more of this.

Later that day, two nurses arrived at my bedside carrying a small tray. They drew the curtains, and asked me to sit on the edge of the bed and take my nightdress and bra off. They were going to apply sticking plaster around my breasts to help with the feeding problem, they said. I sat there with my enormous naked breasts on show and they started to unwrap the little parcels of two-inch-wide sticking plaster, or strapping as they called it in hospital. I noticed that there were several rolls of this sticking plaster on the tray they had brought. They asked me to stand and proceeded to wind it around my body and breasts, turning me around as they crossed it over between my breasts and took it over my shoulders and around my body. They continued to do this until there were several layers in place. I was like an Egyptian mummy when they'd finished. 'It'll help you,' was all I could get out of them. I knew nothing about anything so I accepted what I was told, although I did think it would be a nightmare to remove, strapping like that is very strong and adheres firmly to the skin. Pulling off a small piece was bad enough, the yards of the stuff that were wound around me—well, I didn't want to think about it. I wanted more and more to get out of the place.

Babs came to visit me that evening. They'd had a telephone installed at their house and Tom had rung to say he was finishing work early the following day. I told Babs all my woes and that I wanted Tom to come and get me as soon as he could. She'd never heard of anyone having sticking plaster all around their breasts. The frustration of the feeding situation continued. I was distraught, thinking my baby was not getting enough milk, although the two kind nurses assured me they had fed her with a bottle.

'A bottle is much easier for a baby to suck on,' said the kind Irish nurse. 'So, they don't like us to use them because the baby will become lazy and won't learn to suck on the breast.'

'When my husband comes tomorrow, he'll take me home,' I told her. 'And I'll put her on a bottle.'

'Have you got anyone to help you?' she said.

'My sister-in-law, she's had two babies, she'll help me.'

She nodded as if she understood my frustrations. 'That's good you've got someone to help you, but they'll not like that, they'll try to stop you.'

'They can do whatever they want, I'm going tomorrow.'

The following afternoon, Tom turned up. How pleased and relieved I was to see him. He just walked into the ward and came straight to me. He placed a bag on the bed.

'How's it going?' he said.

'Not good,' I said shaking my head. 'I want to go home.'

He nodded. 'Babs told me about it, so I've brought some clothes for you and Alicia. If you get dressed, I'll go and tell them I'm taking you,' he said. He looked at Alicia who was asleep in her cot at the end of my bed. He smiled at me. 'Don't worry, they can't stop us.'

I unpacked the bag and stuffed the few belongings I had into it. My stretchy maternity trousers were large on me now, but they stayed in place. I tried to fasten my blouse over my breasts, but it gaped open between the buttons. I wrapped my thick Aran cardigan around my chest to cover the gap. I dressed Alicia in her own clothes for the first time. To see her in her nightdress, knitted jacket and bonnet, and wrapped in the shawl that Babs had sent, made me smile. Tom was gone for what seemed like a long time. Eventually he came through the swing doors followed by the other kind nurse. He looked serious.

'Are you ready?' he said. I nodded. 'Let's go, I'm not staying here a moment longer, that dried-up old bitch…' he stopped. 'Come on, the van's parked near the back door…'

Matron, the dried-up old bitch, appeared at the ward entrance as he spoke. She came towards us and stopped. She looked at me.

'You must stay here; your baby isn't feeding…'

'I'm not staying here,' I said, picking up my case.

'You must continue to breastfeed,' she said. 'And if you don't, we will know because we are in contact with all the doctors in the area.'

'We're going,' said Tom.

I gave Alicia, all wrapped up, to the kind nurse. It was a tradition that every baby was carried to the exit when it was going home. Usually everyone was smiling and waving, and the staff would be saying things like, 'See you next year.'

The nurse looked at Matron. 'Shall I go down with them?'

'If you must,' said the dried-up old bitch, looking as if there was a bad smell under her nose.

'Don't get into trouble for us,' I said.

The nurse shook her head—*It's all right, I'll do it*. And off we set through the ward. I waved to the other mums, holding back tears. Down the stairs to the back door and escape.

I thanked the nurse and asked her to thank the other kind one for me. We hurried to the minivan, feeling relieved to be getting away from there. As we drove along, Tom told me the ward Sister had said he couldn't take us out of hospital without the permission of the Matron. So, he went to see the Matron, who told him he couldn't take us home, and that if he did the hospital and the local doctors wouldn't treat me if I needed anything. He had insisted. She had said that I was nothing more than a schoolgirl and had no idea how to look after a baby. He said he wasn't listening to her speak of me like that and he was taking us home. He had to sign a form taking responsibility for removing me from their care, such as it was. In fact, she couldn't stop us from going. I've never been so glad to get out of anywhere.

Babs was waiting for us at home with Cow & Gate half-cream baby milk, and bottles and teats for Alicia, and the kettle on. I needed to see a doctor as soon as possible as I required medication to send my milk away. It was Friday afternoon, and Babs said we'd catch the 5 pm surgery. In those days, you just turned up at a surgery and waited to see the doctor. Tom took me and Alicia, and we went in together. I was nervous that the doctor might start having a go at me or refuse to help me, but he didn't, he listened to me and asked what I wanted to feed my baby on and what my home situation was. He said I seemed to know what was right for Alicia, and that his wife had had seven children, and had not breastfed any of them.

'Always remember that you are the mother, this is your baby and you know what's best for her.'

I was so taken aback by this after expecting a battle that I didn't know what to say except a mumbled thanks. I was very relieved that I would finally be able to feed my baby daughter and I had the tablets to send my milk away.

Later I spoke to my mother on Babs's new telephone and she said she would like us to go and stay with her and Father. It was nearer for Tom's work and she wanted to look after me and Alicia. On Sunday, Tom and I packed ours and Alicia's few possessions into the minivan and drove to Holcombe Brook to start the next phase of our life.

It was the start of a happier time with Alicia. She enjoyed her Cow & Gate milk and fed well. My breasts encased in the strapping suit of armour were still giving me trouble. I'd given up any pretence at breastfeeding but my breasts were still huge and hard, even after taking the tablets the doctor in Ormskirk had prescribed. After a few days at my parents' house, I went to see my old doctor. When he saw the strapping on my body, he said he'd never seen anything like it, that he couldn't see the need for it, and it could be removed.

'Try soaking it in a hot bath,' he advised. 'It'll be torture to get off.'

Did they do it to torture me? I wondered, but decided not to dwell on that. I just wanted it off and my normal-sized breasts back. It took many attempts to remove it. Even hot baths hardly made it any easier. But I persevered, sometimes picking at it gingerly, sometimes bravely ripping a piece off and leaving my skin red and sore. My breasts began to deflate and return to normal. I wanted to concentrate on looking after Alicia and to feel more confident about feeding her, and for her to gain weight. She had lost more than was usual in hospital. We also needed to find a place where we could make a home of our own.

Chapter 23
Alicia 1963

Alicia had wind like all babies, and sometimes colic. She woke up at night for a feed and didn't always settle back to sleep easily. I became used to the sound of a crying baby and learned all the tricks that parents use to try and calm their babies. Was she still hungry? Did she have wind? Or did she have colic? Walking round with a crying baby over my shoulder, patting her back, feeding her gripe water, was something I came to expect. It was hard getting up in the night and feeling tired all the time. But the intense love I felt, the smell of her neck, the feel of her wispy hair, her fingernails—it all compensated for the tiredness. My mother, although still suffering with pain in her back, helped as much as she could, and I could take a nap whenever Alicia did. As I look back, I see that Alicia gave us all a purpose and brought some much-needed joy and hope for the future into our lives as we lived in that miserable situation with the house. Alongside Alicia thriving and growing, the house was still crumbling, and there were ongoing legal problems that needed to be resolved. It was excruciatingly slow, and negotiations about how much Mrs Hardcastle needed to pay my parents for the house were taking forever. It turned out that she had very little money, all she had was a 1950s bungalow with a front garden consisting of crazy paving and rockeries, full of weeds since Mr Hardcastle died, not far from the spot where I used to access the railway line. Mrs Hardcastle would have to sell her bungalow in order to buy my parents' house. She would then have to make good the inadequate foundations and repair the house. That the house next door was also involved in a lawsuit against Mrs Hardcastle was a further complication that provided yet another reason to prolong the agony. I concentrated on Alicia and tried not worry too much about the house situation, or my parents. It was not difficult to do this. I was busy and very tired. For the first time in my life but not the last, I could hardly believe how much time and energy the tiny little person who had joined us took up. Amidst feeding, preparing feeds, washing nappies with an old-fashioned washing machine with a wringer, shopping, cooking, cleaning, lighting fires and everything else, we all loved Alicia. We found time to marvel at her fingers and toes, at her bluey grey eyes, which were later to become pale green, and at her infectious, gummy smile. I remember my mother, despite her ongoing pain, playing with Alicia, still a tiny baby of a few weeks old, and her calling to me: 'She's smiling, come and see.'

Alicia brought life to our dismal household. We had no time to worry or be ground down by other things. I barely noticed the dilapidated state of the house anymore. As she lay on her back in her pram or on a rug kicking her legs and smiling, the state of the house was unimportant. I know now how important those early interactions are for babies and their future development, and how, even into adulthood, those early experiences are retained unconsciously in our minds and bodies. As well as warming everyone's hearts, this kind of interaction confirms to the baby—you're here, you're a separate little person, we love you. And when she first giggled, she made everyone smile and laugh.

My father, emotional and sensitive as he was, was moved by having a new baby in the house. I saw him watching her as she slept peacefully in the big pram we'd borrowed from Babs and Dan. He sympathised when we paced the room trying to settle her after a feed, and he touched her hands, smiled at her and gently tickled her tummy as she lay awake kicking and gurgling on her back. Her presence prompted him to speak to me of my own early days and weeks. Over the years I had gleaned from Mother that it been a difficult

189

time when I was born. She'd been advised not to breastfeed me after her caesarean operation. It must have been a fad at the time because that's not the case now. When I was born in January 1946, there was little choice of dried baby milk. Nothing suited me. If I took a feed, I would vomit it back up. I had been a good weight at seven and a half pounds for a baby born a month prematurely. It was just as well. I hardly managed to retain any milk and began to lose weight. And I cried. They had seven months of me failing to eat, crying and probably giving up hope, along with my parents, of surviving. They both thought I would die. To cope with this, they each separately decided that they would not allow themselves to love me, because loving me would make the loss harder to bear. They only told this to each after the threat of my death had gone. When I was seven months old, they discovered a baby milk called Vitasac. I didn't vomit it back. After the first feed I was contented and, from then on, I started to thrive. Mother enlisted everyone she knew to be on the lookout for Vitasac. It was hard to come by in those early years after the War, when shortages were the norm and rationing still prevailed, but somehow they managed to procure enough to keep me going and I survived. As I listened to this story aged sixteen, with my own new baby, I knew it was important. My father, not crying, but looking as if he might, showed his feelings of despair and sadness and finally relief as he spoke of when I began to thrive. I could understand what he said knowing from my own firsthand experiences the intensity of feelings that a new baby brings to its caregivers and how awful it must have been to live through that experience. And this was an experience that I carried with me at the very deepest level of my being. As I was developing my early attachments to my parents, they withheld their love and attempted to distance themselves from me. I see how the quality of the attachments I have made to significant people in my life have been unconsciously repeated. Those early experiences

190

have engendered in me a tendency to push others away and a fear of being close and dependent on others at the same time as desperately wanting them. But it was to be a long time before I learned that.

Part 3

Chapter 24
Gareth 2004

There is an path I've thought of walking up many times, but I have had neither the strength nor the means to do so. Now I feel ready to make that journey, or at least to make a tentative exploration and see where it takes me, and the Internet gives me the means whereby I can pursue it. I hardly dare to think about this idea when it first comes into my mind. But it seems that someone else has the same thought at around the same time. I search for Gareth online. I find him on the website of the university where I know he works. Dr Gareth Evans, lecturer in maths. He has his own webpage on the university website. There's a photograph of him. His clear, grey eyes are shining with life like they always did. I notice that his thick hair is grey, like mine, and that he looks more substantial than he did as a slim teenage boy. I suppose I do too. He looks rather like I remember his father looking. There's an email address. I ring up Roz, who has maintained regular contact with both Cathy and me over the years.

'Yes,' she says. 'He's finally got his life together, I think. Cathy doesn't say much, she's always very protective of him, but he's working in Leeds and living somewhere over there. Just a word of warning… Cathy is of the view that what happened all those years ago ruined his life.'

'I know they blamed me, but I don't understand that, I was so young.'

'That's what I said to her, you were so young.'

I recently set up a Facebook account and the next time I log in I notice that Gareth has given me a 'poke'. Another of those strange coincidences which have been part of this journey. I need no further encouragement; I email him.

I realise that this may be an unwelcome intrusion but due to the wonders of the Internet I found you online and thought I would say hello and, how are you? I tell him a little about my life, that I'm retired, that I spend a lot of time on my allotment and researching my family history, that I have often wondered how he was getting on and where he was.

I wait for his reply, but not for long. The following day he answers. *I don't mind you getting in touch at all. In fact, I'm pleased to hear from you. I've often thought of you and wondered how you are. I have heard occasional news from Cathy or Roz but perhaps you could fill me in on your life. It's been very different from mine, I expect. I did an Open University degree a few years ago and then I decided to do a PhD. I did it here at Leeds and then I got a job as a lecturer. I only work two days a week, so I travel from Hebden Bridge where I'm living now. As you probably know, I never married and have no children. I still like walking, and trains and railways, that's not changed. You could add IT to that list of hobbies now.*

Do you still go walking? I write back. *I love walking too but I haven't done any for a while. There are lots of walks near Hebden Bridge, I used to take my children there, and to Heptonstall, in the school holidays…*

Gareth and I arrange to meet in Manchester for a coffee. He's already at the café when I arrive. He stands and smiles, it feels strange and awkward. I sit down and study the menu, although I know I only want a coffee. A vacant-looking young waitress takes our order, an espresso for him, a cappuccino for me. We look at each other for longer than would normally be considered polite. I notice that his grey eyes are as shiny and bright in real life as on his photograph. He has a university lecturer's grey beard and he's wearing a sweater that's seen better days.

'How are you?' he says.

'Okay, I'm okay,' I say. 'What about you?'

'Yeah, okay too.'

The coffee arrives, he looks at it and then at me. 'What's this?'

'An espresso,' I say. He looks blank. 'That's what an espresso is nowadays, were you expecting something like we

196

used to get at Chez Odette in the 50s and 60s? A frothy white?'

'Shows my ignorance,' he says. There's an awkward silence.

'I'll get you another,' I say, trying to catch the waitress's eye. 'Do you want one like mine?'

'Yes, thanks.' He smiles. 'I don't buy many coffees, I just drink instant at home.'

'I spend quite a lot of time drinking coffee in cafés with my friends these days,' I say. 'I love being retired.' There's another awkward pause and I have a feeling that this is very different to his life.

'I work part-time,' he says. 'Two days a week at the university. It's what I should have done a lot sooner, but anyway I got there in the end. I still like walking and exploring, especially old railway tracks.' I nod and there's another silence as we drink our coffee. We catch each other's eyes and smile.

'You know I was sent down from Oxford,' he says eventually. I nod, Roz has kept me up to date. 'I kept failing my exams, I didn't do any work. They tried to help me by suggesting other courses and I switched to medicine, then architecture, but I didn't want to do any of them.' He pauses and looks at me. 'You see, I found alcohol. My brother, Russell, found religion when he went to Oxford and I found booze. We were neither of us equipped to cope with university—you know, being away from home.' He gives a wry smile.

'So, what did you do then?'

'Not much, I ended up becoming a surveyor, but it was only a way to earn some money, I wasn't very good at it. I spent most of my time drinking. I just muddled through I suppose, until I decided I should stop and take control of my life. I was a drunk. I don't drink now.' He is looking down as he speaks, but lifts his head and looks at me. His gaze is intense. 'Do you think I'm a wimp?'

'Oh, my goodness, no, of course not, just the opposite,' I

say. My heart goes out to him, he's had a struggle. 'Was that when you did your degree? I mean when you stopped drinking?'

'Yes,' he says. 'I stopped drinking, did my degree with the Open University and then, well, I started drinking again. I drank for a year, then I stopped and did my PhD.'

I tell him about my life, or at least some of it, I can't blurt it out like he did, I can only tell my story bit by bit. We plan a walk and decide to meet the following Saturday to climb Holcombe Hill, his favourite walk and our old haunt.

I meet him in Manchester at the station, where we have a coffee. We both seem more relaxed this time, looking forward to the walk. I've brought my car, so I drive us to Holcombe Hill. It's a fine spring day with a light breeze, but rain is forecast so we're kitted out with waterproofs. I park at the Hare and Hounds, and we walk up the steep cobbled road beside the pub. I'd forgotten how steep it was—I need to stop every so often to catch my breath. There are fields on each side of the track, and a few ancient stone cottages are dotted around at intervals. It's years since I was here but it's all vaguely familiar.

'Oh, the old sanatorium,' I say as we reach the impressive large stone building set back off the road.

'It's a Muslim boarding school now,' he says. 'A Madrassa, sign of the times.'

We stand and look through the big gateway. A sign next to the gate gives us the history. It informs us that it was originally a private house, but it became a sanatorium in the days when people spent weeks or months in these places, where they were treated for tuberculosis. It was part of the National Health Service up until the 1970s.

Up and up we climb until we are almost at Peel Tower. I remember him telling me all those years ago that it was a monument to Robert Peel, the founder of the Police Force. It looks different, the stonework has been repaired and cleaned up. We sit with our backs against a drystone wall on a convenient ledge of rock. There's a good view of the tower above us while we eat our sandwiches and drink coffee from the flask I brought.

'How long have you been single?' he says.

'I'm still married, but we've been separated for four years,' I say. 'I had a relationship with someone else, but it didn't work out. I asked Tom for a divorce, but he didn't want to—so—well, that's how things are at the moment.' He looks at me. 'Tom fell out of love with me. It was painful to be with someone who didn't want me, my self-esteem hit rock bottom and I was getting more and more depressed, so I left… it's not been… easy.'

'I think that's a brave thing to do,' he says.

'What about you? Have you never been married or lived with anyone?'

'No, there've been a few… not many and I've always lived alone…'

'I've thought of you from time to time,' I say. 'My marriage was not without its difficulties. I remember in the early 1970s, when my children were all young, feeling stuck with the way my life was, my parents had both died, my mother when I was twenty-one, and my father, and my brother John, a few years later. I often wondered about you. I remember there was a moment when I gazed up into the sky and silently asked the cosmos where you were. I had a sense that you were a long, long way away from me, unreachable at that time.' I pull myself up. 'God, what do I sound like?'

'That must have been when I was doing the hippy trail,' he says. 'In the 1970s I went in a van with three other guys overland to India, and then to Australia where I worked in a mine for a while before I came home… How amazing that you had a sense of me being far away.'

'Yes, I definitely had that feeling,' I say. 'Things like that happen to me at times.'

'Shall we carry on up to the tower?' says Gareth.

I notice again how huge the tower is when you're close to

it. There's a locked door on one side. We walk around its four walls and look at the views over the Pennine Hills. The sky suddenly clouds over into a uniform grey.

'I think it's going to rain,' I say. 'Perhaps we should make our way back.'

He suggests as we drive that we stop off to see his parents' old house. I agree. Why not? There are some old ghosts that need exorcising and a visit to the old house might help. It's only a few minutes by car. I swing left into the avenue and it's immediately obvious that there are changes. The railway line has gone, and new houses have been built where it lay, and where we once trod its sleepers. I drive around the bend of the road to the end of the avenue where Gareth's old house is. It's been extended and modernised. I park outside. We sit in silence and look around us. A bungalow faces his old house, sitting squarely on the spot where the railway line once passed by. There are several detached houses built all along where the railway line used to be. There's a new frontage to his old house, and heavy, pale curtains are draped in the window of the front room. The front garden is immaculate, designer plants, box balls and a gravel path are elegantly arranged. We look at each other.

'It looks a bit… twee,' I say. 'Overdesigned.'

'It's certainly different from when we had it,' he says.

'Do you still want to go in?'

'We can't come so far and not knock on the door,' he says.

'Okay, let's try.'

We knock and wait. Footsteps approach and the door is opened by a slim woman in her forties. She's elegantly dressed in designer jeans and a creamy cashmere sweater. Her hair is shoulder length, blow-dried into a blonde bob, and she has perfect light make-up. We stand in silence looking at each other.

'Yes?' she says. 'Can I help you?'

'Hello,' says Gareth. 'This is a bit odd.' He glances at me.

I smile to encourage him. 'I used to live here, in the 50s, and... well, we've just been up Holcombe Hill... and we were in the area... we sat outside in the car and thought we should knock on the door, and...'

She smiles and visibly relaxes, realising that we pose no threat, two oldish-looking people taking a trip down memory lane.

'Would you like to come in? You can have a look around if you like, it's probably changed quite a bit since your day.'

She is chatty and friendly, obviously proud of her house and its décor. Most of the ground floor has been extended and is hardly recognisable. Big picture windows look out onto the back garden, and the kitchen is huge. Everything is light coloured, cream or pale grey, and immaculate. The only room that is remotely the same is the front room. Our room.

'We use this as a study,' she says. 'It's just the right size.'

We both enter the room and stand looking around. The walls are painted a tasteful light beige colour, there's a modern cream desk in the corner where Russell had his desk, and a couple of pristine, leather armchairs. A large photograph of three smiling blond-haired children hangs on the chimney breast. The old fireplace has gone, replaced by a wood-burning stove in a stone surround. We look at each other and smile.

'This was our room,' says Gareth. 'We did our courting in here, but it does look different.' I start to giggle, 'courting' sounds such an old-fashioned word. I'm slightly hysterical.

'Oh, look at the time,' says the woman. 'I'm going to have to go and collect my children from school...'

'We must go too,' says Gareth.

'I don't want to rush you...'

'No, no, it's fine,' I say. 'It was kind of you to let us look around.'

We say our goodbyes and go to sit in the car. We turn to each other and shake our heads.

'It's awful,' he says. 'So sterile, I can't believe that children

201

live there.'

'Very tasteful,' I say pulling a face. We laugh.

We arrange another date. I agree to go to his house so we can walk from there. I'm curious to see how he lives now. I'm wondering where this is going to lead us, what am I wanting from him? Am I sizing him up and for what? A friend? A partner? A lover?

Following his directions, I find his house easily. It strikes me that it's in a setting very much like his parents' house. It's a short cul-de-sac with small detached houses on one side, and opposite the houses a railway line runs parallel to the narrow roadway. Gareth's house is perhaps thirty or more years old, with a small front garden and a garage, although he doesn't have a car. He opens the door, welcoming me with a smile. Inside there are two rooms and a tiny conservatory which looks out over a small back garden. The furniture in the front room doesn't match the carpet and curtains, which came with the house. An old lady had lived there until she went into a home. He inherited the décor and the carpets, and someone gave him the sofa and chairs. It looks old-fashioned, stuck in the 1970s. The walls are lined with bookcases, which contain his collection of maps and his books, which seem to be mostly about trains and railways. A large desk against one wall is covered with more books and papers. He doesn't have any decent tea or coffee, so we drink instant. He tells me he lives on ready meals, the cheapest he can find as he must be careful with his money. He's not well-off. He says the women on the checkout at Aldi know him as someone who can manage to buy a great deal of food on a small amount of money. I swallow down the hint of nausea I feel at the thought of cheap ready meals.

My life with Tom had been very different. For the first ten years or so we had very little money, and our life was domestic—children, animals, holidays in caravans in Wales and the Lakes. We lived in a tiny rented cottage for two years. As Tom's business prospered, we moved from our next house—a small semi, bought on a mortgage with a £200 deposit borrowed from my father—to a detached house Tom built for us. We enjoyed better holidays abroad, renting villas in Portugal and Menorca. We shared a love of good food. We ate out in good restaurants and enjoyed the best of fresh food at home. Gareth hasn't done these things. Food is of no interest to him. The common ground we have is the past and an enjoyment of fresh air and walking.

We sit together with our instant coffee and reminisce. He's been looking through his photographs and found some of me. There's one where I'm wearing denim shorts sitting on a boat with my legs sprawled out. My mother is standing nearby. We must have been on holiday. On the back he's written 'Mrs Cox and Beth'. I had photographs of him which I got rid of when I left home and married Tom. Tom was jealous of my relationship with Gareth, not to the extent that it caused problems, but I thought burning the photographs would be a sensible thing to do. I didn't want to keep them, I wanted to forget what had happened. Yet here I am nearly fifty years later, sitting with Gareth, talking precisely about that time I tried to forget. There's a photograph of Cathy and Tessa, his sisters.

'Roz told me that Cathy thought it was my fault, that I led you astray?'

'It was no one's fault,' he says. 'We were both up for it.'

'Some people would say it was down to you, as you were older than me, and in the eyes of the law you were the responsible one.'

'What do you think?' he says, looking at me.

'It's something I've often thought about,' I say. 'You led the enterprise, but I could have stopped it—I didn't, so I think we were both to blame—that's if you want to apportion blame—which is probably not a helpful way forward.'

He nodded. 'Your father questioning me, 'What have you been doing to Beth?', that was awful—then he came to see my father…'

'What did your father say?'

'I don't remember, not much, they packed me off to Oxford and my parents moved to Wales, they both drank a lot, you know...'

There's a silence. He takes hold of my hand, our eyes meet, we lean towards each other and we kiss. I move away.

'I'm not sure...'

'It's all right, don't worry, we won't go there,' he says, his voice is kind. We sit for a quiet minute. 'Have you brought your walking boots?'

I nod. We fuss about putting on our boots and waterproof anoraks. I check my backpack for the sandwiches and flask although I know they are there. He checks he's locked up everywhere and we stand on the path outside his house. He gets out a map and shows me the route he's planning to take me.

Chapter 25

Losses 1967–1978

Tom has been a part of my life since we first met in 1961. We don't live together now but we maintain regular contact. He visits me, usually to help with a household or allotment chore that needs more muscle than I have. I cook him a meal. He appreciates that, as the woman he lives with isn't a good cook. Tom doesn't know I'm seeing Gareth. Over a long period of time, all that happened has faded into the background, but I suspect that if Tom knew about Gareth, it might disturb him.

In the early days of our marriage although money was tight, I would have liked to have had another baby when Alicia was two, but we decided to wait until we were older and had a place of our own and more money. Instead, I decided to do my nurse training, which lasted for three years. In 1965, my parents' legal battle about their house was finally settled. Mrs Hardcastle sold her bungalow and, through solicitors, an amount of money as payment for my parents' house was finally agreed upon. My parents didn't come off well with this deal, but they were relieved to be done with the problem, which had caused them so much worry and ground them both down. They were satisfied that they had enough money for the much-longed-for bungalow in Kent. Father applied for jobs and quickly found work as a salesman in a furniture shop in Sevenoaks. He and my mother lodged in digs for a few weeks while they searched for and then bought a property. My mother was fifty-three and my father fifty-five. For a time, it looked as if life might go well for them, but Mother was never free from illness. She still suffered from back pain, made bearable by high doses of painkillers. She couldn't walk far, and she was slow. But they found a small bungalow in Tenterden and managed to put a home together. That phase of their lives was short-lived as my mother's health deteriorated. She went into the Middlesex Hospital in London for further surgery on her back. She became less mobile and in more pain after each of her many operations. She was in hospital for weeks on end and my father's ongoing mild depression and psychosomatic symptoms spiralled down into a severe depression. He was admitted into the Maudsley Psychiatric Hospital and was there for several weeks. He did not respond to treatment, which was medication and basket-making, so they gave him electro-convulsive therapy and discharged him. He never fully recovered. His daily dose of librium enabled him to lead a limited life. He could drive and slowly perform a few tasks. He was also diagnosed with Parkinson's disease and chronic bronchitis around this time. My poor mother, now paralysed and using a wheelchair, arranged for their bungalow to be sold. We borrowed £200 off them as a deposit for a house near to Tom's work and they gave us some of their excess furniture. What was left of their possessions went to a tiny flat in Bolton, part of a development owned and managed by the Masonic Lodge. I hadn't understood when my father explained to me as a child that being a member of the Masons was an insurance policy, but now I saw that he was right.

Tom and I, and Uncle George and the aunts, Elsie and Lizzy, all helped to settle Father into his new home. He was barely capable of washing and dressing himself, and could do nothing towards unpacking his and Mother's, by now, very few belongings. By that time, I was a student nurse in my third year of training, and I agreed to collect my mother from London, and bring her back north on the train. The journey had been arranged by the hospital almoner, who would accompany Mother in the ambulance and hand her into my care. I was to take an early train and wait at Euston Station for Mother to arrive in an ambulance from the Middlesex Hospital. I waited for about an hour at Euston until they arrived. The almoner greeted me with a sad smile and gave me a large bag. Mother was carried on a stretcher to the train. The almoner told me that everything I might need was in the bag and if it became impossible to manage Mother at home, it might be possible for her to go to a hospice. As hospices were a new idea, they were few and far between. The nearest was in Yorkshire. I decided then that I would look after Mother myself. I would take time off work if necessary.

Mother was gently placed by the ambulance crew so that she was lying across the seats on one side of the train compartment that had been reserved for us. Train carriages in those days consisted of a corridor with compartments off it. Each compartment consisted of bench seats facing each other, so it was possible to recline across the seats. I arranged the pillows behind her head. She gave me a weak smile.

'Are you comfortable?' I said, pulling the blanket over her.

'They gave me an injection,' she said. 'I'm fine for the moment.' She closed her eyes.

I sat down opposite her and looked in the large bag I had been given. It contained a bedpan, a bowl and a small bucket with a lid. A few gauze swabs and tissues, a bottle of water, her toiletries and her nightdresses were in another bag, along with her medication, and a note for me. The note informed me that she'd had a shot of diamorphine before she left the hospital and could have another one if necessary four hours later. She could also have Brompton Mixture, which was a bottle of oral medicine which contained morphine and other pain-relief ingredients. There were other medicines as well, but I knew that the diamorphine, which is heroin, and the Brompton Mixture were only used for terminally ill patients. My mother was dying. My eyes filled with tears. I looked across at Mother lying, facing me with her eyes closed.

I gazed at my mother. I'd seen her about a month previously when I'd travelled down on one of my days off to the Middlesex Hospital. Since then, her pale face had become more drawn. Her lovely hands and arms looked thinner, and when I helped her to use the bedpan later, I could see she had lost weight. She was very thin. I was exhausted. I'd worked a twelve-hour night shift at the hospital the previous night, so as Mother slept and dozed, I did the same, lying on the seating facing her. I roused myself to help her when she vomited, needed a drink, and when she needed to use the bedpan. In 1968 the journey from London to Manchester took well over three hours. An ambulance was due to meet us at Manchester and take us to the flat in Bolton. That could take up to an hour. She was restless and in pain towards the end of the journey, so I gave her another diamorphine injection to help manage the rest of the way. It made her vomit, but she soon settled again. The ambulance was waiting for us. The men handled my mother with care as they placed her on a stretcher. The drive took about an hour and, thanks to the diamorphine, Mother slept most of the way.

Father's flat was on the ground floor of a small block that had been built in the garden of a large house. It was close to our old house in Bolton. The ambulance crew carried Mother through the gardens on the stretcher and placed her in one of the two single beds in the only bedroom. Father met us. He too looked thin and drawn. District nurses had been arranged to help care for Mother. Neighbours, friends and relatives helped as best they could. It was April 1968 when Mother arrived back in Bolton. She limped on, bedfast, hardly eating, in pain, but conscious and alert until the last few hours of her life in July 1968. I spent as much time as I could with my parents. One day, Mother initiated a conversation when she told me that she knew she was dying. She said she was content with how her life had been. She had travelled quite a lot for those days, and she said I'd turned into a very capable girl. She wished John would find a nice girl and settle down, but she knew he would be all right. She asked me to look after my father as he was in such a bad way. I said I would, through my tears.

My annual leave coincided with her final days. We cancelled our holiday and I went over every day, staying the last night in the flat, dozing on the sofa. Father dozed on his bed. We knew the end was close; Mother lost consciousness, faded and passed away the following morning. She was fifty-five years old. John had been visiting her regularly as he now lived back in Bolton, but we couldn't find him until after her body had been taken to the chapel of rest. He arrived at the flat and burst into tears. I, who had been strong, in nurse mode until then, cried and sobbed with him.

To write this is hard. Even now, so many years later, the pain of it suffuses my mind and body, my whole being. How unbearable it was, how I absorbed the hurt of it, and how much I missed my mother, especially when I became a mother again myself. I went on to have two more daughters. One was born the following May, Miranda, then, three years later, Rebecca. Those babies helped me to carry on. Because there was more sadness and loss to come.

Father was left alone fending for himself. He managed to drive his Mini, albeit very slowly, causing other drivers to become frustrated. He came to my home every week for a meal and to bring his washing, which I did for him. His routine was to stay in bed until early afternoon, then he would go out to eat in the evening. He had one or two cafés he liked to go to, and his neighbours, fellow Masons, were kind to him. He regularly collapsed on these trips out and had to be rescued. On one occasion he'd driven himself to a Methodist holiday home in Blackpool. He hated it, it was too cold, the food was awful, and he demanded to come home. Tom and John had to go together to collect him and his car and bring him back. He complained all the time of aches and pains, and often called his doctor out. His doctor was patient and kind. Father cried a lot, nothing was right for him, and when he came to our house, he would turn off any music or television that was playing, without asking anyone if he could. The children, doing their piano practice or watching television, found him frustrating. It was never warm enough for him. He would only eat certain foods. He wanted to come and live with us. I did what I could to help him, but he tried my patience and I had to say no to that request. John would have nothing to do with him. John also came every week to our house for a meal and he too usually brought his dirty linen with him, but on a different night to Father. John and I became closer during these years. He loved Alicia and Miranda, playing rough and tumble games with them, and getting them overexcited before bedtime. Everyone loved John. Feminists have talked about the role of women in families—an idea that women's roles can be used as metaphors for the emotional life of the family. The metaphor of washing the dirty laundry is apt here. I processed the dirty linen. I had the role of making it clean for everyone. I was the one who tried to manage the feelings in the family, tried to process them and make them acceptable. I think I did that for my great-grandmother, Elizabeth, and I did something of the sort for myself too. I didn't see it like that at the time, but I do now.

It was a Monday, 14th December, 1971. I was five months pregnant with my third child. John's birthday was 13th December, and I had been trying to contact him over the weekend to invite him for a birthday meal. He hadn't answered his telephone. I wasn't at all worried about him because I knew he had a new girlfriend, Jenny, and I thought he must have been spending time with her. We would catch up during the week. Monday was the night Alicia went to Brownies at the local church. I went to collect her afterwards. When Alicia and I returned home and entered the house, I knew that something had changed. The atmosphere was thick, charged with a feeling I couldn't name. Tom had been putting Miranda, our two-year-old to bed. He came downstairs as we came through the kitchen from the back door, and we met in the hall.

'Robert has been on the phone,' he said. 'Robert—as in Cousin Margaret's husband—asking if we've seen John.'

'I've been trying to contact him all weekend,' I said. 'Has something happened?' The phone rang, I moved to answer it.

'I'll get it,' said Tom. 'You take Alicia upstairs to bed.'

I could hear Tom speaking quietly into the phone, which was in the hall, while, upstairs, I took Alicia through her bedtime routine and tucked her up.

'Can I have a story?' she said.

'Not tonight, but you can read to yourself for a little while,' I said. I left Alicia sitting up in bed with a book open on her lap and went downstairs to where Tom was sitting in the lounge. I sat down. We looked at each other.

'What's happening?' I said as my stomach turned over.

'Well… the thing is,' he said. 'We don't know… that was Robert again. There's a rumour going around Bolton, that John or your father is dead.'

'A rumour… I don't understand…' I said. The phone rang again. Tom jumped up. 'I'll get it.'

I heard again his voice, quiet and serious, his ums and ahs, and 'I sees' into the receiver, then putting down the phone and standing in the doorway. His face set and sad.

'I'm so sorry,' he said. 'It's been confirmed by the police, it's John.'

I couldn't believe it. Little by little we found out what had happened. I don't remember who told me what or when, but John had died on his 34th birthday, Sunday 13th December 1971. The last person to see him alive was his girlfriend Jenny, who had been out with him on Saturday evening. He lived in a farm cottage on a country lane in Westhoughton, near Bolton. The woman who lived next door noticed that his car was parked outside all day on Sunday. On Monday morning she went in to clean the cottage, which she did every week. She thought he'd left his car and got a lift to work as he'd recently had some problems with it and had left it parked up the previous week. She cleaned downstairs and then went upstairs. In John's bedroom she found John, face down on the floor in his pyjamas. Stone-cold dead.

She couldn't find any details of where I lived or my telephone number in his house, and nor could the police, although she knew he had a sister. In the end the police found my father. We had to wait for the post-mortem to tell us what had happened. No foul play was suspected, nothing had been stolen, he'd just died. My handsome, big brother who loved life, and who loved to make people laugh, who loved my children and who could make washing-up an occasion for fun and laughter, had gone. I cried a lot for a long time. I cried when I was peeling carrots, when I was washing up and sometimes completely unexpectedly as I walked down the street. In the early days I heard the back door open and his voice as he came inside. Our back door was always unlocked and often wide open. In the days when dogs and children played out all day, it was open for Alicia and for Janie, our Dalmatian, to come in and out whenever they wanted to, even when we were out. And I don't mean I *thought* I heard John, I believed I did hear him. I saw him on television, and walking down the street, and I looked for him everywhere. It was different from the loss of my mother, and of my father, which followed four years later. They were older and their deaths were expected, although I know now that I didn't grieve properly for them at the time. It was only much later that I allowed myself to grieve. But I did grieve for John. I went to see his body in the chapel of rest because I believed they had made a mistake. But they hadn't. He was dead and I saw the line of stitches on his head where they'd stitched him back together after they'd sawed through his skull to examine his brain at the post-mortem. I still harboured thoughts that it wasn't him there, that it was someone who looked like him, while at the same time knowing that it was him.

John was distant from me for much of my childhood, and as I grew up, he was often absent. But as we grew older and we knew our mother would soon leave us, and our father was difficult, we clung together. He loved my children and they loved him. Tom and John were friends. For a very long time after his death I thought about him every day. My life was filled with children and housework, and I worked one or two nights each week as a nurse. Tom worked long hours; I wished I had the freedom that he had. How I envied him his Christmas drinks with his workmates while I sat at home and mourned my losses. Even though I was so busy, I thought constantly about John, I didn't stop thinking about him for years. How we got through, I don't know because Tom's mother, Mary, became ill with dementia in her late fifties and his father, Ken, had a life with his new wife and her family that didn't involve us much. We did make it through those years, but only just. I recall thinking one day that it had been some time since I'd thought about John. That I had come through it. And that was seven years after his death.

John died of cardiomyopathy. He had a diseased heart. No one had any idea, he was a sportsman, he played tennis, cricket and football. Many years later, a new young doctor at my local practice picked up that I had this history and sent me to the family history clinic at Manchester Royal Infirmary. I had a heart scan and an ECG. Everything was fine. It must have been a genetic mutation they said, an aberration. No one else in the family had anything like it, it was just another of those things.

My father seemed less affected by John's death than I imagined he would have been. It was almost as if it was just another thing for him to complain about and be sad about. But on reflection, it must have made him feel even worse, if that was possible. His life was one long round of misery and no one could help him. The last six months of his life were spent in a nursing home. He was miserable there. It was too cold, and they wouldn't turn the heating up. The food was uneatable, they didn't give him his pills when he should have had them—everything was wrong. He was very slow and frail during those last months. He died four years after John. To me it was as much a relief as anything. I was sad for what he had become. I had lost my real father many years ago, before life ground him down. I'm eternally grateful for the anti-depressant medication that's available in the present day, and which saved me from a fate like my father's. I always defend medication when people argue against it. It has its uses and should be valued for what it can do. My father had twenty years of a half-life full of misery, which affected not only him but his family and others around him. Others with mental illnesses often had it worse.

When I started therapy in the 1990s, as I was required to do to become a therapist myself, I spent a great deal of time crying. It was for the loss of my parents, less so for John as I had grieved for him at the time, but I had put the loss of my parents to one side as I got on with my life, a large part of which was being a parent myself. I was needy but frightened of closeness after so much painful loss, and this is what Tom and I went through, and what drew us back together, all that and of course our children. Who else can you boast about your children to? Who else can you sound off to about your children? And who knows that however much you complain about them you still love them? It is only the other parent that those things can be shared with. It was the shared history of those events and those people, our parents, our extended families, as well as our experiences of relationships with others, which both of us had found disastrous. It was all these things that brought us together again, and a willingness to change, to learn from our mistakes, although there would always be new mistakes waiting for us to make.

Chapter 26

Melling. Then and Now 2004

Before 1834, when it became compulsory to register births, marriages and deaths, these events were recorded by the church. As a result, there can be difficulties with these records, although some are digitalised and available through local or national archives. They are handwritten, sometimes in Latin and in old-fashioned script, which can be a problem for modern eyes to decipher, especially if you're reading a microfiche. They may be faded or damaged and some have been lost or may not even have been recorded at all, as it depended on the vicar or curate to ensure it was done correctly.

To find further details of my family before 1841 is therefore a welcome surprise. I discover that John Cock, my great-great-great-grandfather was born in Halton, near Lancaster. It's another uncanny coincidence, as this village was home to my eldest daughter, Alicia, for a few years. In fact, she lived in a house near Halton Green, which was exactly where John Cock's family lived. Alicia's was a newish house so not the same house that the Cock family lived in, but maybe the same spot. Who knows? John's parents were Robert Cock and Catherine, née Proctor. His brothers and sisters were Richard, Margaret, Elizabeth, Mary and Elin. They were a family of farm labourers so John's elevation to schoolmaster stands out again as remarkable. This information is taken from parish records available on the Internet. They detail the baptisms of John Cock and his siblings, and the marriage of his parents. There seem to be no records of the family going back any further, but there are several other families in the surrounding villages with the surname Cock. This group of people in what was Lancashire and Westmorland is the second largest with the surname Cock in the United Kingdom. The largest group is in Cornwall.

I can go no further, nor do I need to; I have found what I was looking for. It's something intangible, a visceral sense of being vindicated, and it's connected to the story of expectations and hopes that started with John Cock, a boy from a family of farm labourers becoming a schoolmaster, and how his son William's good fortune at becoming a clerk at the Ship Canal Company was changed by the tragedy of baby John Robert, born with hydrocephalus, who died aged seven months on Christmas Eve. It's connected to John's son William's downfall, dying young, leaving behind six children and a wife, living in the Britannia Street slum. It's connected to Elizabeth Margaret, my great-grandmother, who disgraced the family further by bearing two illegitimate children. I cannot imagine what she went through, what judgements were made about her, I only know what I experienced in 1962, and that was bad enough. Her legacy was transmitted to me, her shame was kept secret—but traces of it were palpable—she'd been labelled and so had I. Tragedy can breed more tragedy. Once on a downward spiral it's hard to reverse. In my father's family, a hidden sense of shame was always being fought against, a sense of having to do better than the previous generation was always in the background, and loss and grief pervaded our lives for years and years. We are what our family history makes us, both consciously and unconsciously, the tentacles of unresolved issues from the past reach into our lives in the present. The secrets and lies of hypocrisy and snobbery, now seen for what they are, have begun to free me from the shame and humiliation of the past. Now we think nothing of babies being born out of wedlock, and people live together openly without condemnation. Enough small changes in attitudes by individuals and society made together over a long enough time frame can cause seismic shifts to happen for the better.

It has been such a privilege to meet my relatives, to see their lives in handwritten copperplate on my laptop screen. It was my job. I've always known from childhood that it had fallen to me to unpick the past, face it, look at it, study it, and apply my learning and understanding of people and life to it. It was something I knew I would do. It has helped me to be kinder to myself, less ashamed and less judgemental. Carrying secrets is stressful, it shapes a family and the family members are touched by it in ways they don't know.

I tell Gareth about my family history research and something of what it means to me. He's interested, so we decide to have a day out to explore Melling and the surrounding area. It's where Great-great-grandfather William and his family were living in 1841. I drive and we set off early. It's June and the morning dawns bright and clear. We're both in good spirits, there are no traffic hold-ups on the M6 motorway, and I fill Gareth in with more family stories and explain further what it's meant for me to discover what happened to my great-grandmother and her illegitimate children. I mention that three-times-great Grandfather John Cock was a collier at one point in his life and that he must have worked in one of the coal mines in the Lune Valley. Gareth is fascinated by that and interested in exploring that area.

We drive through Lancaster and I point out where Britannia Street was and the church the Cock family attended. I'm feeling excited as we leave Lancaster behind and drive into the countryside. Melling village is just over eleven miles from Lancaster. The road is quiet; this is very different from the Lakeland hotspots of Windermere and Ambleside. As we enter Melling, we look for somewhere to park. There's a village hall on the left, the church, St Wilfred's, formerly St Peter's, a few yards ahead on the right, and Melling Hall facing us in the centre. We park near the house Crow Trees, to the left of the Hall. It's a house I remember from the census form. I turn to Gareth.

'It's such a strange feeling to be here,' I say. 'Walking in my ancestors' footsteps, I feel so emotional about it, rather like I did when I found all the records online.'

He takes hold of my hand and we look around. The church is visible on our right, but the old vicarage is hidden behind shrubs. It's a private residence now. The church noticeboard has details of the vicar, and the dates and times of services held there. It tells us that the vicar is a woman. She oversees a handful of parishes and conducts services on a rota. So different to what the Reverend Tatham's responsibilities would have been in 1841, when the vicar and the church would have been central to the life of the village, and when there were no women vicars. We turn our attention to Melling Hall on the other side of the road. It's a large and surprisingly gracious house. It looks as if it would be more at home in Jane Austen's Bath than a small Lakeland village. It dominates the village as it must have done in the nineteenth century. There's building work going on at the hall and we chat to the builders, who tell us it's been divided up into three properties. They're working on the last one, which is nearly finished, and people have moved into the other two parts. It was a hotel for a while, so this is its latest transformation. We walk round and see the land at the back of the hall divided up into gardens. It all looks very smart with landscaping, lawns and box balls everywhere.

We walk through the village along the lane. It's very quiet as we move away from the builders. In 1841 over two hundred people lived and worked in Melling, and that number hasn't changed much, although there are now no shops and no pub. There's a new primary school at the far end of the village, set back off the road. The old Victorian schoolhouse in the centre of the village is a private residence. I stand back to look at it. It's such a charged experience to see where John Cock, his wife Anne and their children lived and worked. I imagine the village being much busier then. The forge would have flashed and roared as horses were

218

shod. I found in my research that a coach and horses travelled twice a week back and forth from the appropriately named Horse and Groom public house in Melling to the Red Lion, a large pub in the centre of Lancaster, not far from Britannia Street. If they didn't use horsepower, the people of Melling would have walked to Lancaster. It's unlikely anyone would have commuted daily to Lancaster as I imagine they might now. The church, the vicarage and the school (it was and still is a Church of England school) would have been at the heart of life for the villagers. We explore all around the village, but there's no one about and very little to see. A walk around the graveyard beside the church doesn't reveal any Cock family graves. But I'm thrilled to be here, it's a lovely place, I'm pleased that for a time my ancestors lived here and prospered.

We sit in the car and look at the map. Gareth points out to me that Wennington, where the coal mines are, is closer to Melling than Millhouses, where John Cock lived for a while when he was a collier, so we decide to go there first. As we arrive in Wennington, another small, quiet village, we see the railway station on our left. We use its car-parking and peruse the map. I notice that Blands Farm is very close by. I tell Gareth I'd read that there had been a fire at Blands a few weeks ago in which the resident, a shepherdess, had died. The article had briefly alluded to the myths and legends that had grown up around this house due to some unusual features in the garden, and to the activities of a previous owner, Arthur 'Perpetual' Burrows, who was famous in the area in the nineteenth century for trying to invent a perpetual motion machine, and for mining coal from the cellar beneath his house. I tell Gareth about the trapdoor in his kitchen. Gareth laughs.

'It's probably empty,' I say. 'Shall we have a look round?'

'It's too fascinating to ignore,' he says.

A sign takes us into a lane leading to Blands Farm. The fir trees at each side of the lane have been hacked back. They look a mess. As we reach the end of the lane, we see the burnt-out shell of the house on our right. The roof has been destroyed apart from a single, charred wooden beam hanging over the space beneath. The stone walls are blackened by fire. We walk up to it and stare at the scene of devastation.

'That was some fire,' says Gareth.

'Terrible to think someone died in there.' I shiver and turn away.

'It must have spread quickly,' says Gareth.

As we move away, a tortoiseshell cat comes to greet us, its tail held high. It fusses around our legs. There is a stone patio in front of the house, messy with old plant pots and weeds. This leads down some steps to a lower area and further on towards an overgrown lawn and garden. At this lower level, brambles and elderflower shrubs hang over a full and fast-flowing stream. We wander through the lush grass. I feel like a child exploring a magical kingdom and, like all the best fairy tales, there's a creepy sense of darkness as if something evil lurks behind the next hawthorn bush. A full-size wooden door is set in a wall which appears to lead under the lane that runs to the site. Gareth pulls on the door and we peer inside. It's not possible to see far into this tunnel.

Turning away from the tunnel and back into the garden, we see on the far side a huge pond or small lake, empty apart from a puddle of water on the concrete base. A small, decrepit, upturned boat lies at its edge. We walk around the shell of the house and find there is a neglected orchard, surrounded by a belt of fir trees at the back. A large barn stands to one side. Nearby is a dilapidated greenhouse. We make our way around to the front of the house, where we sit on the low wall and eat our sandwiches. We both notice a rusty sign hanging on the broken gate—*Nirvana*. I look at Gareth and pull a face.

'How ironic,' I say, but it is a sunny day and as we sit on the terrace eating our sandwiches and banana bread and drinking our coffee with the cat lying purring in the sun close by, the creepy feeling dissipates. 'It doesn't seem hungry,' I say, nodding towards the cat.

'It's friendly and looks in good condition,' says Gareth. He goes to put our rubbish in the dustbin. 'There are a lot of empty tins of cat food in here, someone has been feeding it.'

He stands back, looking at the house. 'I wonder if it's for sale,' he says. 'It could be at a knockdown price because of the state of it—just my kind of project.'

'I'd love to get my hands on a garden like this,' I say. 'I miss having a garden.'

We walk away from Blands to explore nearby Clintsfield Farm, where the remains of an engine house and mine workings should be visible in one of the fields. It's not far and, following the Ordnance Survey map, we easily find the extant buildings and remains of the mine. A farmer is driving a tractor through the field and he stops and shouts to us, do we want something? Gareth says we're only looking at the remains of the coal mine. The farmer says to take care and goes on his way. The coal mine area is a fenced-off hollow and the remains of the machinery and the pit head are visible. I stand and stare, affected by this discovery of the place where I think John Cock may have worked as a young man. If he did work there, did he sustain an injury that stopped him from undertaking physical work and enabled his transition to village schoolmaster? I can only speculate, but I feel close to these ancestors, a real connection.

John Cock lived in the hamlet of Millhouses, within easy walking distance of Clintsfield. This makes me even more certain that Clintsfield was where John Cock worked. There are a couple of, probably, twentieth-century houses here and a cluster of ancient cottages. We walk past them, looking and wondering if one of these was where John and his family lived. Did he keep hens and grow vegetables in one of the long plots at the back of the cottages? As I stand looking at the cottages, I feel a shift in the atmosphere, a fracture in the fabric of this world, and I know that the middle cottage, number 2 Millhouses, was where John Cock lived.

Chapter 27
Tom 2005

Tom comes for lunch. I tell him I'm thinking about my future and of possibly moving from my flat into a house with a garden. I've missed being able to walk straight out of a back door into my own outside space. This means we will have to arrange our finances so I can have the remainder of my half of our joint estate. It raises the question of divorce again. We're sitting at the kitchen table drinking coffee. I look at him. At his familiar face and form. I'm overwhelmed with feelings and tears well up.

'I don't want to divorce you,' he says. There's a silence.

'Tom, I'm sorry,' I say. 'I needed to... have space, I needed to find who I am.' I dab at the tears with a tissue and put my clasped hands on the table. He leans over and puts his hands on mine.

'It's all right,' he says. 'It's all right.'

We sit like this in silence for a long minute. I look up, smile and slide my hands out from under his.

'I lost myself...'

'I've always loved you,' he says. 'But I didn't love who you became.'

'I was depressed, and neither of us realised.'

'You're better now,' he says.

'Yes, I am.'

'I needed space too,' he says. 'I needed to see how I could manage alone, but I didn't like being by myself, that's why I'm in the situation I'm in.' He grimaced. 'It's all wrong.'

'Sandra?'

He nods. We sit quietly again for a minute or two. I get up.

'How about another coffee?' I say.

'Please.'

The last walk with Gareth set off a train of thought

about the future, my future. Spending time at Blands Farm, as fascinating and enticing as it was and as much as I want to create a garden—and the garden at Blands was as interesting and full of potential as any could be—has focused my mind on what I want now and where I want to be. I know that I don't want to be in a small village in the middle of the countryside. I want to be right here, exactly where I am, in this Manchester suburb where I've found myself. I value the life I have. The friends, the cafés, the restaurants, the fact that I can walk along the high street and buy a bottle of milk, a newspaper, some fresh fish, cheese from the cheese shop, a cup of very good coffee—in fact, more or less anything I want—without having to drive to find it. I would like a garden… and I would like someone to share it with. Gareth has never shared his life with anyone. He has no children and doesn't see much of his family. He doesn't seem to have any friends. He's talked about his father's meanness with money and I see something of that trait in himself. It's partly because he doesn't have much, but it's more than that. It's a feeling I have that he wouldn't spend money even if he had it. Our lives have been very different. I'm glad we've reconnected; it's laid some ghosts. He's always been there at the back of my mind with a sense that we had unfinished business together, that he was waiting for me. Both of us had held on to a vague idea of us being together. Maybe it helped us, supported us to live our lives, to survive and to endure what life threw at us. Both of us were too frightened and ill equipped to go out in the world. He'd anaesthetised himself with alcohol; I'd buried myself in marriage, childcare and work. Being with Gareth would not be right. Without speaking directly about this, I know that we both know this. We've experienced a taste of how it could be and we both know that it never will be.

The more I think about this, the more I realise that the only person I can imagine sharing my life with is Tom. Tom is married to me but he's living with Sandra. He says he shouldn't have asked her to live with him, she's not right for him, but he hated living alone and his loneliness took over his better judgement. He tells me she's always felt threatened by me. She knows that he loves me, that he will always love me, and she feels second best. Am I thinking of Tom because of my loneliness? And as much as he says he's unhappy with her, when it comes to it, it is quite another thing to leave her. Perhaps what I need to come to terms with is being alone. At the root of mine and Tom's problems was the difficulty of being together. We were good at giving each other space but being close was often a problem. Tom kept me at a distance, and I see now that I did the same thing with him. If we moved closer an argument would often follow which served to create distance. But within that dynamic is a latent potential for cooperation. There is no doubt we're a great team when we do work together. Would he be willing to go for help if we needed it? We had help previously, and it was beneficial. I'm stronger and better placed to have a relationship now. I know who I am, and I know that my feelings are valid. I know what's mine and what belongs to someone else, what's relevant and what isn't. By that I mean I won't let Tom, or anyone else, persuade me otherwise. I won't be fobbed off or treated badly. I need support at times, but I'm not overly needy, just in normal need of support from a husband or lover. I expect to be listened to and in turn I will listen. I can be tolerant and cut some slack at times. I want to be put first (most of the time), before work, before hobbies. That doesn't mean that these things can't be a priority sometimes, but I must feel loved and cared for and cherished. I hadn't expected to think about my future in quite this way. Is this a reasonable list of needs and wants?

Our marriage had been about children, about a home with a family and with animals, a home with life in it. It's no coincidence that in the years running up to me leaving Tom, our children had all left home. The oldest two a few years before, then our youngest Rebecca, who had been to university and came back home to live with us again as she was working in Manchester. I loved having her at home. I went to the cinema and theatre with her, and I enjoyed her company. What alerted me to something wrong in this was the loneliness and devastation I felt when she, quite rightly, told me she was going to flatshare with friends. I realised I had been relying on her too much.

Animals had also been a big part of our lives. There had always been a cat and usually a dog or two. And for a couple of years Miranda had a pony. We had, over the years, goldfish, terrapins, koi carp, gerbils, rabbits and a budgie. Tom and I loved animals, and so did our girls. Over a couple of years before I left Tom, we had lost a young and beautiful chocolate Labrador with a tumour in her chest, our beloved and naughty Jack Russell, who (unbearable thought) went down into a badgers' set and never came out again, and our sleek and athletic Burmese cat, who had to be put to sleep. It had been truly heartbreaking for us and we were left with just the two of us. What would our relationship be like now that all these children and animals had gone? I had felt that I was the only one considering this question, the only one trying to find a way to stay together, to find a new way of being. I felt unloved, uncared for, unwanted. I could no longer continue to live that way. I made a conscious decision to withdraw my love from Tom; I stopped trying to make it work. There was nothing left, and I became, ever so slowly, depressed.

That isn't the whole story and I'm sure that Tom has his own view on that time. But what I am sure of is that we both needed to be out of the relationship and alone. We needed to see what we could do, what we were capable of as individuals, and most of all we needed to find ourselves, to know who we each are. We had never had time alone in the world as teenagers and young adults, we had jumped over that into parenthood and the trappings of adulthood, but the basis on which our personalities had developed was not strong. Like my parents' house, the foundations were

226

inadequate. We'd been bolstered by the trappings of adulthood, children, houses, animals, but we needed the space of six years to do the psychological work we had leapfrogged over as teenagers. In my case, I had been ill equipped to go out into the world by myself as a teenager, my foundations were inadequate then. Too many traumas, large and small at that time, made me scared and weakened me further. I couldn't see a way through it, and I couldn't wait to move away from the ongoing traumas of my parents' ill health and misfortunes. When I've spoken to Tom about this, we've both agreed that we were probably suffering from a low level of depression as teenagers, maybe even before, and making a family was in fact a creative decision. One of my therapists spoke of it that way, and I like that way of thinking of it.

Chapter 28
Towards the end

It's a satisfying thought that at the end of my family history research, I have achieved something of what I set out to do. I hoped to discover what happened in Lancaster all those years ago and, while there are still unknowns (who was the father or the fathers of Great-grandmother Elizabeth's children; what did Elizabeth's father William Cock die of; what caused his serious, or serous apoplexy?), it's unlikely I will ever discover the answers to these questions. Not knowing who my great-grandfather was is far enough back in my history for it to leave only a small void. Many of the pieces of the family jigsaw puzzle have been placed in their rightful positions, and I believe I have discovered what changed the fortunes of Elizabeth's family. I feel Elizabeth was maligned and misunderstood, both in her lifetime and in the following two generations whose lives, I believe were stalled, not fully lived, and that this was influenced by the legacy of their Victorian parents' upbringing and the class system and women's roles in society. The two world wars shook the world and set the scene for change in society. The repressions of the past began to loosen but it required another generation to pick up the emotional legacy of the past. The next generation's narrative is engendered by the previous generations' story. And it landed on me to let in the ghost of Elizabeth. This was signposted by Elizabeth and I sharing a name and a birthday. I believe that telling this story has liberated energies held back by the previous generations. I hope I have managed to change the perception that the family had of Elizabeth. Sadly, I will never be able to explain to my dead relatives what I have discovered, but if any future generations are interested, they can read about her life and the times she lived in and not judge her too harshly.

I also was compelled to explore those four years of my life from the age of twelve to sixteen that shaped my life profoundly. I hoped to gain some perspective on that time from the distance of forty to fifty years, and to form a deeper understanding of myself. I have been lucky enough to live long enough to be able to do that. This insight is predicated on previous therapeutic interventions which had prepared me to be open to further understandings. Discovering what happened in Victorian Lancaster from a distance and in the context of present-day mores and values, as well as in the context of the time and place in which they happened, has helped me to relate to experiences in my own life, view them from the distance of the present and achieve a new perspective on them. The act of writing down my story and that of my namesake, Great-grandmother Elizabeth Cox, has given me—literally—a new view on those events. Seeing the words on the page, reading them and potentially sharing them has had an astonishingly therapeutic effect. As a young girl, I was impatient to experience everything, but I could also be shy and out of my depth easily. I'm allowing myself to see how this and the family circumstances at the time led me into trouble. I'm aware of my own damaged psyche and the shadows that the past has cast upon it. I needed to know that teenage part of me that I'd tried to ignore and thereby integrate it into my personality.

As I look back, I know that my life was in many ways good when I was a child. I never lacked a roof over my head, although both my home and my family became unstable during my adolescence. I was never hungry; I ate good enough food; I was clothed; I was given the opportunity of an education, which was considered the best in the area where I lived; my parents were good people, they did their best for me; I was loved. But I was damaged, sensitive and poorly equipped to cope with life's challenges. My life veered off its predetermined course and I was unable to deal with it. My parents, broken by events and poor health, were unable to help me and guide me during my adolescence. I ran wild, although by today's standards it was a tame wildness, and I was plagued by guilt and remorse afterwards at making my parents' lives worse, and at the shame I felt I'd brought upon the family.

Adolescence is a precarious time when emotional separation from parents is an important developmental task. It works best when parents are robust enough to take the attacks that can be mounted on them by their teenagers, who may be at the mercy of conflicting forces—both wanting and not wanting to separate emotionally. If parents are weakened, as mine were, the task may be complicated for the teenager. I believe that this was the case for me. I effected a separation in a dramatic way by forming my own family. I needed desperately to find a way to escape from the life I had and to protect myself from the lurking but barely conscious fear of my parents' deaths. The fact that I was so determined not to end my pregnancy shows this. Adolescence and teenage years are the times when we start to find our own way in life—which group do I belong to? Where are my kindred spirits? What is it I am passionate about? It may take time to find the answers and a young person needs a secure enough base to explore from. Or if they are not strong enough to exist in a state of not knowing by themselves, that's when it's possible to become lost.

Writing this memoir has shown me how hard I have worked to put distance between those four years of my adolescence and myself as the person I became when I married at sixteen. I worked and studied almost continuously as well as having a husband, and three children to bring up. This left an unacknowledged and unintegrated part of myself behind. I needed to know about and accept the teenage Beth. It's the part I was ashamed of and felt guilty about. The six years when I was separated from Tom gave me space to explore and discover that part of me. This memoir tells the story of one aspect of those years. This teenage Beth has been brought into the light, looked at, accepted and forgiven. This was no easy task and writing this memoir has highlighted my difficulties with this. I kept speaking and writing about myself in the third person, as Beth or 'her'. Now I consciously think about this and make the effort to say 'I'. In this way, the Beth part of me has been slowly integrated into my psyche and I am more of a whole person as a result. It's impossible to describe the feeling, but I'm calmer, stronger, more myself. Although this came about recently, it was based on my whole lifetime of experience and learning. It is greatly informed by my years of study and practice of psychoanalytic psychotherapy, and the remarkable patients, therapists, supervisors and teachers with whom I've worked.

One of my aims in undertaking this research and writing this book was to gain a deeper understanding of how I ended up as a pregnant teenager. Every pregnant teenager has her own story. She has her own family (or lack of it) and the context of the time and place she is in. She has, as a fertile young woman, an opportunity to use her body in a way that will change her life. She is reminded every month when she sees her menstrual blood of the potential for creating a baby that her body holds. A baby can give purpose and hope to a girl whose life seems lacking in those things and who can see no other way forward. With a baby comes the potential for change. The experience of pregnancy and childbirth will change a woman. Becoming a mother will have a profound psychological effect on any woman, whatever age she is. It is a life-changing experience.

In my case, it was not just external events but my own psychopathology which caused me to behave as I did. Early life experiences are considered crucial for normal development. We now know that our brains and our psyches are wrought from our earliest moments. Our relationships with our early caregivers can set an unconscious template that can cause us to behave in certain ways. Psychoanalysts and other writers describe a complex range of vital interactions that take place between the child and its early caregivers, resulting in the child developing the first sense of its separateness and the basis of a sense of self. We have no conscious awareness of this and no memory of those early days, months and years, but the experience is carried in our bodies. This is something that therapists have always thought to be the case, and now we have neurological evidence. The first seven months of my life were spent in a state of hunger and despair. My parents could not allow themselves to attach and love me. They thought I was going to die. Instead of a thriving, contented child, they had a crying, hungry baby. This must have been a desperate time for everyone. I think it left me without solid resources deep inside me. My parents' ill health when I was a teenager was, I now believe, much more terrifying to me than I consciously realised. I feared abandonment, not consciously at the time, but I believe it propelled me towards making a family of my own to mitigate against the fear of being left alone. The losses which came when I was in my twenties were devastating and the impact of those resonated for many years to come. People cope with loss in different ways and as I struggled and put a brave face on life, it impacted on my family and my relationships. But although damaged and depleted at times, I had some reserves of strength and energy, and I soldiered on until Tom fell out of love with me and I left him.

For people of our generation—Tom born in 1943 and me in 1946—there has been a lot to adjust to. Our parents were the products of Victorian parents and large families. They continued to live and bring up children informed by their own Victorian upbringing. Except for birth control and perhaps the chance (at that time) of more opportunities to have a better standard of living for the working classes, their ideas were based on the old model. They were enmeshed in traditional roles. The man was the breadwinner and the woman was the support, although of course there were always variations of that basic and generally accepted model. During the War, my mother ran the business. My father never saw active service during the

War, but he was away from home, based in Kent with the Royal Electrical Mechanical Engineers, or REME. Mother and John managed without him in Bolton. When he came back, everyone had to adjust to the way life was before the War, except that lives had been changed and adjustment was not always natural or easy. This must have increased the tensions between John and Father. There are clearly Oedipal issues here which left a lasting impact on their relationship. As well as his resentment at his treatment by Father, I think John never forgave Father for coming home and breaking up his closeness with Mother. Father's subsequent treatment of John did not help John deal with that.

The wider society and culture impacts on any child's development. I was born in 1946. My birth must have been accompanied not only by the hope that most newborn babies bring with them, but coming as I did after two world wars and at the end of the Second World War, I'm sure I embodied heightened hopes for the future, in this land 'fit for heroes'. My parents had both gained scholarships to their local grammar schools. My mother was not allowed to take up her place at Pendleton Girls' High School because her older siblings had not had that opportunity. My father did attend Bolton County Grammar School, but the story was that on his sixteenth birthday, his father asked him how old he was and when he replied, Grandad said: 'It's time you were working, lad, don't go back to school.' And that was that. Any hopes of an education were frustrated. Both my parents thought that by giving John and me the best education possible, we could fulfil our own and everyone else's dreams.

So much was changing in post-War Britain. I believe that our parents were unprepared as we hurtled from the drab and dismal 1950s towards the 1960s, and the social revolution that followed. We were going to break free! There was a lot of sex, free love and drugs, then the pill. Women began to assert themselves and question the paternalistic values that had held sway for so long. Some men have had to be dragged kicking and screaming through this, as men's and women's roles were no longer clear cut. Younger men nowadays no longer expect to be waited upon, cooked for and have their washing done for them. Men of Tom's generation have fallen between two stools; the older generation, who thought as their fathers had done, that power and authority over women was their right (if they ever thought about it and probably many didn't as the system worked in their favour), and the younger generation, who generally accept women as equals. It is of course true that this is a generalisation and that there are still many more changes needed on the theme of women's rights and equality. Tom and I fought some of these battles on a personal level.

Tom and I found each other when both of us had experienced our lives going off course. We have been an important part of each other's lives ever since. Now, we are committed to spending the rest of our lives together. It has not been an easy ride at times, we have had some difficult moments, but we want to be together, and I know it is the right thing. In our seventies now and living through worrying political, health and ecological crises, and both having lived through cancer, we intend to make the best of these years that we have been so fortunate to reach. As people who are very different in some ways, with diverse interests and hobbies, it is our love for each other, our family, our home, our animals and our shared past—these are the ties that bind us together.